Monographs Personal And Social

Baron Richard Monckton Milnes Houghton

1 2

(Houghton
— A

115

IN PREPARATION.

MONOGRAPHS

POLITICAL AND LITERARY.

BY

LORD HOUGHTON.

SULEIMAN PASHA.

MONOGRAPHS

PERSONAL AND SOCIAL

BY

LORD HOUGHTON

NEW YORK

HOLT & WILLIAMS

1873

FROM AUTHOR'S ADVANCE SHEETS.

Stereotyped at the
WOMEN'S PRINTING HOUSE,
56, 58 and 60 Park Street,
New York.

DEDICATION.

TO

GEORGE STOVIN VENABLES, Q.C.

HISTORY is the summary of biographies, and I must appeal to the indulgence of a forty years' friendship in submitting these biographical sketches to the attention of so complete a historian of the past, and so acute an historical critic of present times.

But if you, for reasons of your own, have selected the vehicle of the anonymous press for the communication of your large and accurate knowledge and the exercise of your vigorous and humorous judgment, it the more becomes those who have long known and followed your literary course, to remind your weekly and daily readers to whom they owe so much solid learning, and so much agreeable illustration.

The artistic form of biography, in which the personality of the portrait is made subservient to the skill of the painter, and which from Tacitus to Johnson has charmed mankind, is now classed with romantic fiction, and shares the fate of the old decorous history that has fallen beneath the arms which Niebuhr forged for our youth, which Carlyle and Lewis have wielded with gigantic force, and with which men of the intellectual diversity of Froude and Freeman are still contending against dear tradition.

It is therefore difficult to determine in what shape it is best to preserve to after-times the deeds and words of best or better men. To throw before the public what in a brute material sense may literally be called their Remains is the easiest and most common process, and, whatever may be gathered together by affectionate and discriminating hands, much is properly left to the vultures and beasts of prey.

Yet it seems to me that a truthful impression may be produced by a combination of general and personal observation, which, while it leaves the characters in the main to speak for themselves, aims at something like a literary unity of design. And when, as in the greater part of the following notices, this interest is cemented by individual sympathy, there is a chance of the production of a more than transitory record.

Although I am not aware that in these pages the personality of the writer is unduly prominent, I am not sorry to have this opportunity of vindicating the advantage of an intimate personal relation between the describer and the described. It may indeed sometimes give to the reader the sense of a double purpose, which damages the integrity of the work; but far more is gained by the consciousness of the sincerity of an affectionate interest than is lost by the exhibition of any casual vanity, which is often but the reflex of loyal admiration.

I am reminded by your own faithful and pathetic memorials of those you have loved and regretted, how much you could have added to one at least of these monographs, but I have preferred strictly to adhere to my own apprehensions of character and impressions of words and things, so that I might remain solely responsible for what is here related as having been said and done.

HOUGHTON.

CONTENTS.

———•-•-•———

SULEIMAN PASHA.

WRITTEN IN 1846.

DURING that strange episode of the French Revolution the siege of Lyons, a wealthy tradesman of the name of Selves was one of the most active defenders of the independence of his native city against the tyranny of the Directory. His eldest child, a boy of about seven years old, brought his daily food to the ramparts, and grew inured to the fierce game of war. When resistance became useless, and the infuriated conquerors took possession of the devoted town, it was not probable that Citizen Selves would escape a vengeance which honoured no courage and respected no submission. He was accordingly soon summoned before a tribunal composed of the most savage partisans of the central authority, and having been denounced by an old acquaintance, was on the point of being led to execution, when one of the judges, to whom Citizen Selves had happened to have shown personal kindness, asked him whether his accuser did

1

not owe him some money.   Selves asserted the fact
to be so, and the friendly judge contrived to represent the accusation as a trick of the denouncer to
avoid payment of a just debt.   The attempt succeeded—yet, that the *auto da fé* of liberty might
not be cheated of a victim, the court substituted the
plaintiff for the defendant—and Selves at once
obtained his own freedom and ample satisfaction
on his prosecutor.   But the boy who attended his
father on the walls well remembered the scene of
domestic anguish—while the mother, believing
herself a widow, sat weeping among her children,
and would not be comforted, till the well-known
knock at the door roused her in an ecstasy of astonishment, and she fell into the arms of the
husband so miraculously rescued.   And her dark
hair, blanched by those few hours of mental agony,
remained as one of the many tokens of that im-
partial tempest which spared neither the most
elevated nor the least obtrusive classes of society.

Thus early initiated in the severest realities of
life, the boy grew up, and soon desired to take his
share in the mighty battle which France was then
waging with the world.   The profession of the
navy was open to everyone who passed the
requisite examination, and young Selves was ad-

mitted as *aspirant de marine*. In this capacity he
showed great intelligence and undaunted courage,
and was engaged in that conflict which Napoleon
announced to his council as 'the loss of some
vessels by the severity of the weather, after a
combat imprudently engaged in,' but which we
English remember as the Battle of Trafalgar. He
was on board the vessel from which the shot was
fired that mingled a nation's sorrow with a nation's
triumph, and years afterwards he recounted the
circumstances of the death of Nelson to those who
escorted him, an honoured guest, over the battered
hulk of the 'Victory.'

A short time afterwards the midshipman Selves
fought a superior officer in a duel, at Toulon, about
a lady, and had the misfortune to give a fatal wound
to his adversary. Fearing the consequences, he
determined not to return to his ship, but to try and
seek employment in the Army of Italy, then
flushed with triumph, but glad to receive young
and vigorous recruits. He passed several regiments
till he came to one of light cavalry which he
thought would suit him, saw the commander, and
frankly told him the story of his desertion ; his
former captain, when applied to, verified his state-
ment, and what is more, interested himself to get

him formally transferred from the one service to
the other, which was effected without much difficulty. Soon after his enrolment in the regiment
it became necessary to instruct the cavalry soldiers
in infantry practice, and young Selves' knowledge
of the exercise was of the greatest use and brought
him into general notice.

The incidents of a life which is all adventure are
rarely recorded, and though the old soldier would
gladly relate how his commission and his cross
were won, and though he has a tale of every field
and an illustration for every page of that wild and
varied volume of the world's work, it is from his
own lips they should come, narrated with epic
simplicity, and full of the hero-worship, the self-
sacrifice, and the unconsciousness of that great
pagan episode of modern history.

During the Russian campaign he acted as aide-
de-camp to Marshal Ney, and saved his own life in
the retreat by judiciously buying a fur pelisse from
a soldier at an enormous price.

After the occupation of Paris, in 1814, he submitted unwillingly to remain in the army, but was
one of the first to join the standard of Napoleon
the following year. You should hear him tell the
story himself. He was quartered at Lyons, his

native town; the regiment was ordered out for inspection; the commanding officer announced to them the escape of the late Emperor from Elba, depicted the evils that would ensue, and energetically called on them to preserve their fidelity to the Bourbons, and protect their country from the desolating ambition which had brought it to the brink of ruin. Nothing was said, but glances were exchanged, and soon after Colonel Şelves and other officers found themselves on the road towards Grenoble. There was a cloud of dust, and out of it rode the well-known form, and the magic voice uttered, 'Ah, Selves! je vous reconnais; est-ce qu'on m'attend?' 'Partout, Sire, partout!' and Selves followed him to Waterloo. During that fatal day he was on the staff of Grouchy, and urgently represented to that general the propriety of joining the main body of the army as soon as the Prussians, whom he had sent to intercept, were out of sight. Had this juncture been effected, it would, indisputably, have greatly influenced, and a Frenchman may believe might have altered, the event of the day.

On the second restoration of the Bourbons so zealous an Imperialist was naturally set aside; and finding himself, in company with a large body of fellow-officers, in an equivocal and disagreeable position, he proposed to the Government to give them a ship, and allow them to form a colony in some of the islands of Oceania; the charms of Taiti having even then captivated the French imagination.* The proposal was rejected, and then Selves set out alone, determined to find fame and fortune in some less ordered and civilised community than that which now hardly owned him as a citizen. The name of Mehemet Ali had already become known to Europe as that of a successful proconsul who had not only by a combination of subtlety and courage destroyed one of the most regular and powerful military organisations that ever tyrannised over a subject country, but was attempting, by the introduction of European discipline and policy, to give a new value and character to the land and people of Egypt. The dynasties of Napoleon and Kleber had left behind them that tradition of strength so grateful to orientals, and, as a distinguished officer of the Great

---

* Taiti has long been an Eldorado in France. Poor Camille Desmoulins, writing to his wife the night before his execution, reproaches himself for having mixed in these tumultuous scenes, being far more fitted by nature to form a Taiti of peace and happiness with those he loved.

Army, Colonel Selves received a hearty welcome, and was at once offered high rank and sufficient emoluments in the army of the Pasha, while the tact he showed in allowing himself to be sent into the deserts of Horeb and Sinai in search of gold mines (for the easterns easily attribute to an European the most diverse and inconsistent knowledges) raised him at once in general estimation.

He soon informed the Pasha that if he wished to possess a force fit for an European officer to command, it was still to be created, and having obtained all he required to be placed at his disposal, he repaired to Upper Egypt, and there passed between two and three years, literally forming the Egyptian army. The docile Arab, though as blindly attached to his mud huts and palms beside the Nile as ever the Swiss to his snow-topped mountains, recognised the intelligent teaching, consistent discipline, and calm forbearance of the French commander; and when Colonel Selves returned to Cairo, he presented Mehemet Ali with an army of whose steadiness and skill the sovereign of many an European state might be proud. Once invested with this new instrument of strength, Mehemet Ali lost no time in using it, and when

Arabia no longer offered a field for its exhibition, and Greece had won its independence, a quarrel, ingeniously contrived, with a hot-headed minister of the Porte enabled him to meet the Turkish army in fair battle, and to make himself master of the whole of Syria. During these campaigns Colonel Selves was the presiding genius, and the title of Suleiman Pasha was the homage to his success. The army was under the nominal command of Ibrahim, the eldest son of Mehemet Ali, but it was clearly understood between them that from the first shot that was fired Suleiman became pasha, and Ibrahim his lieutenant. The battle of Koniah especially brought out the strategic powers of Suleiman, and showed him a worthy pupil of his great master. It was won by a movement on the flank of the enemy, and this difficult and delicate manœuvre, in which the French had failed at Rosbach, but in which Frederic the Great succeeded at Kolin, and Napoleon at Arcola and Austerlitz,* ended in the total defeat of the Turkish army, and opened to the Egyptians a clear road to Constantinople. But in vain had Mehemet Ali triumphed at Koniah and at Nezib; in vain had the troublous

* To these instances may even be added the decisive attack of the Prince of Prussia at Sadowa.

and energetic population of the Mountain been, for the first time in history, deprived of means of resistance ; in vain did the mosques of Damascus resound with the name of Sultan Mehemet in place of Sultan Mahmoud. Diplomacy had discovered that this conflict could not continue without risking the peace of civilized Europe, and, by the interposition of European force, the Egyptian army was arrested in its march of triumph, and the dreams of Mehemet Ali's independent greatness were at an end. Yet, while the English fleet was in the act of bombarding the Syrian fortresses, the overland mail from northern India and Persia, by Bagdad, was intercepted by Suleiman : he took out the consular dispatches which bore upon the war, read and burnt them, and forwarded all the other letters to Admiral Stopford under a flag of truce. The return mail was expedited in the same way, and thus the generosity of Mehemet Ali to the great mercantile interests of the world found its fit complement in the courtesy of his lieutenant. Of so much value was the presence of Suleiman Pasha in the enemy's ranks estimated that, by the Turkish Government, and through the English admiral, offers the most gratifying to ambition and avarice were made to induce him merely to retire

1*

from the Egyptian service; the government of
Crete, accompanied by a very large sum of money,
was one of the inducements proposed and rejected.

After a painful retreat through the desert, encumbered with a population of followers, for whose
wants Suleiman provided as if he had been com-
missariat-general, he arrived at Cairo, only to per-
ceive that the edifice of military power which he
had raised with such untiring patience and energy
had crumbled to pieces, and that he was left with
the reflection of what, under happier auspices, it
might have been.   The versatile mind of the Pasha
took refuge in visions of indefinite industrial wealth,
which his successors, and especially the present Khe-
dive, have gone far to realize ; the carefully trained
cavalry were sent up the country, and used for ordinary agricultural purposes, while the soldiers became
labourers of the lowest kinds of toil.   The wealthy
repose enjoyed by Suleiman in his luxurious palace
on the banks of the Nile, and the general consideration acquired by his skill, vigour, and beneficence,
were a poor compensation to him for a project
which would have changed the face of the earth,
and the destiny of millions of men—the foundation
of a great Arab empire, which should be within
the reach of all European civilization, and act as

mediator between the eastern and western world. Having mixed little in politics, even at the time that his arms were deciding their course, he has had still less inclination to do so now his especial function has ceased; and by this prudent abstinence he has kept clear of all the intrigue and deception which are inseparable from eastern state-craft. Contented with a position the right to which none can dispute, he has no enemies, for he has no rivals, and he can afford to succour the weak and protect the oppressed. He has made out of his harem a veritable home, and his wife is an object of unbounded envy to the Egyptian ladies for the respect with which she is habitually treated. She was a Greek of good family, taken prisoner at the siege of Tripolizza. He purchased her from her captor, and found her a willing and useful servant, and she him so indulgent and considerate a master, that when the prisoners were liberated after the battle of Navarino she preferred remaining with Suleiman to returning to her family. He rewarded this choice by making her his wife, and he has never taken advantage of the legal permission to have more than one.

To strangers generally, and especially to French and English, the house of Suleiman Pasha is

opened with a cordial hospitality; and one who
brought away from it pleasant and grateful recollections has attempted in these pages to leave some
memorial of its interesting possessor.

He is, in truth, an admirable specimen of that
type of man so little known in this country, and
yet so worthy of observation, a real soldier of the
French Empire. The Restoration, like all other
periods of forced and unwelcome government,
degraded the vigour and tarnished the simplicity of
this phase of national character, and made rare
that spirit of unconscious devotion, of idolatrous
patriotism, to which France had been as much, and
Napoleon more, than ever were Rome and Cæsar
to the legions. This feeling, so distinct from
national vanity and admiration of power, never
possessed a human breast more absolutely than
that of Suleiman Pasha; admitting no comparisons,
it requires no jealousy to defend it; refusing all
criticism, it implies no injurious deductions, no
perversion of right or blindness to wrong. This
idiosyncrasy requires to be seen to be understood,
at least by Englishmen, in whom the military spirit
is something accidental and alien, and who never
worship heartily either a man or an idea. The
feeling of the Irish towards O'Connell is the nearest

approach to it in our time ; and in France it is only to be found where the soldier of the Grand Army has retired from active life and subsists upon his memories. There was little of it to be detected in the metropolitan crowd that received the ashes of Napoleon ; but I have seen it in remote villages, where the old soldier has become again the peasant, and, after having helped to change the face of the world, recovers his little portion of patrimony, and has no more selfish pride about what he has done than an old crusader would have had for having recovered Jerusalem. I remember seeing in a Norman village a half-pay captain, who had fought from Fleurus to Waterloo, enjoying his cider and cake of buckwheat, as contented as an English officer at the United Service Club.

This peculiarity certainly forms a great charm of the society of Suleiman Pasha, but his shrewd observation and practical sense would have made him distinguished in any class or time ; while his great benevolence and humanity are really astonishing in a man who has gone through so many scenes of strife and suffering. For he has preserved his feelings so uncorrupted by all this contamination that he invariably speaks of war with pain and repugnance, and seems forgetful of none of its

horrors, though he has shared in all its glories.   An
Austrian officer, of the name of Durand, tried to
cut off the supplies of food from the large and ir-
regular body of Egyptians, including hundreds of
women and children, with whom he was retreating
over the desert in 1840.   'If I had caught him,'
said Suleiman, ' I would have hung him before the
whole army ; as if war was not horrible enough
without these infernal resources of diplomacy.'

In 1845 Suleiman accompanied Ibrahim Pasha
to France, and brought his son to be educated at
Paris.   ' He might be a great man in the East,' said
his father, ' but I can make him nothing but a
Frenchman.'   When Ibrahim came to England
Suleiman accompanied him, and, during a short
visit, interested and delighted all the public personages and men of letters with whom he became
acquainted.

There was one subject to which no one would, of
course, refer but himself—namely, his adoption of
the Mohammedan religion.   He, however, does so
frequently and always apologetically, and prays his
hearers to remember what was the religion of the
Revolution and the Empire, and not to judge him as
one who had known the full truth of Christianity.
' Ah ! ' he would say, ' si vous saviez ce que c'était

la religion de l'armée dans ce temps-là, vous trou-
veriez que j'ai beaucoup gagné en devenant mussul-
man. Quand nous étions dans la Terre-Sainte, on
se demandait, " Pourquoi ce nom-là ? " On n'avait
pas l'idée de l'histoire du pays.' To the eastern
Christians both in Egypt and in Syria he has been ·
of essential service, and, though bearing the name
of a renegade, has been covered with the blessings
of the rayahs protected from pillage, violence, and
persecution.

The only parallel, I believe, in modern history
to the subject of this sketch is Count Bonneval,
Achmet Pasha. He, too, distinguished himself by
feats of arms in the war of the Spanish succession
and under Prince Eugene, and, having betaken
himself to Constantinople, was received by Mohammed V. with great honour, and conformed to the
religion and institutions of Islam ; but here the
resemblance ends : Bonneval's life was one of
flagrant profligacy, only relieved by dashing
bravery ; he fought against his own country, and
tried to betray that which he had adopted : his
excesses drove him from France and made him a
State prisoner in Austria ; and he only retreated to
the East when banished from Europe. He held,
indeed, high office in the Turkish service, but was

prevented from effecting the only object he attempted—the reformation of the artillery—by the jealousy of those in power, and easily consoled himself by a life of unbridled licence. There is nothing in this description in common with the entire loyalty, the unblemished honour, the chivalrous zeal, the sagacious prudence, the simple habits, and the generous disposition of Suleiman Pasha.

I have only to add to the above delineation of a very interesting man that he came to England once again shortly after the commencement of hostilities that led to the war in the Crimea. 'Vous prendrez Sébastopol,' he said, ' mais il y aura des œufs cassés.' He went by special invitation to the Reviews at Boulogne, where he was received with great distinction by the Emperor. It was not the first time that they had met. The portrait attached to this memoir was drawn on the occasion of his first visit to this country, by that eminent artist M. Gudin at a picnic in Richmond Park, where Prince Louis Napoleon made one of the party. I remember well the interest the Prince took in the Pasha's narrative of his chequered life, and the invitation he gave him to come and see him in France in happier days—a prognostication wonderfully accomplished.

On my return to Egypt, as representative of the Geographical Society, in 1869, at the opening of the Suez Canal, I saw Shereef Pasha, the Minister of the Interior, who had married one of Suleiman's daughters, and who spoke of the great consideration in which the memory of his father-in-law was still held.

II.

ALEXANDER VON HUMBOLDT AT THE COURT OF BERLIN.

THE annoyance felt by men of scrupulous honour in this country at the supposed breach of confidence in the rapid publication of the correspondence between Alexander von Humboldt and Varnhagen von Ense, and the malicious character of some extracts that have been largely circulated, doubtless prevented many persons from finding in that volume all it suggests and reveals.

Varnhagen von Ense was an indefatigable collector of autograph letters, and he has left behind him one of the largest collections on record. Unlike many other amateurs, he attached the main importance to the characteristic or historic contents of the documents he amassed, and a considerable portion of the work is taken up by contributions received from Humboldt for this purpose. He appears, however, to have had some compunction

as to the retention of Humboldt's own letters to
himself as part of his treasure, and, however much
it might have afflicted him in his dilettante pursuit,
he would probably have destroyed these revelations
of Humboldt's innermost life, had not the writer
himself distinctly expressed his notions on the
subject: 'Make yourself quite easy in the possession of my irreverences (*Impietäten*),' is the sense
of Humboldt's letter of 1841 ; 'when I am gone,
which will not be long first, do exactly as you
please with them ; they are your property.' Yet
on another occasion Humboldt complains of the
unjust historical impression which is conveyed by
accidental and transitory epistolary phrases, and
illustrates this in his own case by a passage in
which Schiller tells Körner that he, Humboldt, is
'a man of very limited understanding, who, notwithstanding his restless activity, will never attain any
eminence,' at the very time that their relations were
of the most intimate character, and after Schiller
had written to him in a former letter that he was
a far more gifted and higher-minded man than his
brother. Humboldt also quotes a letter from a
collection of autographs in Augsburg, in which a
friend writes, 'Alexander Humboldt again accom-
panies the King to the Congress of Aix-la-Chapelle

in the capacity of bloodhound,' and adds, 'Such are the representations on the stage of life for the benefit of a credulous posterity!' He therefore knew very well what he was doing when he authorized Varnhagen to keep his letters, although perhaps he never anticipated that they would appear in any concrete form : he may rather have expected that the facts and opinions contained in them would come out incidentally at different intervals, when the chief actors in the scene might have passed away : but he was clearly willing to take upon himself all the responsibility, without anxiety as to any pain he might inflict or any irritation he would excite.

It is therefore not Humboldt or the friends of Humboldt who are injured by the publication, but those persons of high social and literary station who are roughly and often unjustly criticised. With most of these judgments, however, it is probable that Varnhagen heartily agreed, and his representatives may possibly share his feelings, and there is more literary discourtesy than breach of confidence in any fault that has here been committed. My concern, however, at this moment is with the figure of Humboldt himself as the writer of these petulant and discomfortable letters, and as I saw him at the Court of Berlin in the years 1845–6.

The position of Humboldt at that period was the cause of sincere gratification to all those who loved to see genius successful and rewarded, and also the source of much envy on the part of all whose merits had never been acknowledged either by prince or people as they thought was deserved. His intellectual eminence indeed was so unchallenged, that when he passed from writing a chapter of Cosmos to his daily reserved place at the royal table opposite the King, there was no pretence either of favouritism or of service—it was the fair and honourable interchange of the highest social station and the noblest mental powers; the patronage was on both sides. Who suspected the deep discontent that lay at the bottom of that old man's heart? Who believed that he was seeking refuge from that courtly splendour, and even from that royal friendship, in secret satire and confidential depreciation of all about him poured into the ear of a literary contemporary of whose complete sympathy he was well assured?

And yet there can be nothing in this very new or surprising to those who really understood the temperament and culture of Humboldt, and the character of the society in which he moved. 'Under an appearance,' he writes, 'of outward splendour, and in the enjoyment of the somewhat fantastic preference of a high-minded prince, I live in a moral and mental isolation.' Rahel had said long before, 'Humboldt was a great man when he came to Berlin, then he became an ordinary one.' May not the meaning of these two paragraphs be, that Humboldt at Berlin had always been the Courtier and as such in a false position? In a French novel called 'Barnave' (by the Bibliophile Jacob) there is an excellent character of an old German Baroness, who, having accompanied Marie Antoinette to the Court of France, is at length compelled by the menaces of the French Revolution to return home, and resume her former state and dignity: to her son's congratulations on the recovery of her independence she can only mournfully reply, 'Comment vivre sans servir?' This feeling is incredibly strong in a country where the multiplicity of small courts has enfeebled the self-reliance of the upper classes, and to few Germans would it seem incompatible with any eminence of literary or scientific attainment, or even with perfect consciousness of moral power. There must have been something of it latent in Humboldt himself, or so large a portion of his life would not have been spent in the formalities and requisitions of a courtier's existence.

His royal intimacy indeed had begun with King Frederic William III.; and his relations, both with that sovereign and his court, were happier and more natural than at the period of this correspondence. He himself was younger, and more in harmony with the events of his time. That King, though far inferior to his son in accomplishment and erudition, was a philosopher in his way, and of a school which tended to results not far different from those familiar to the thinkers of the eighteenth century. This tone of mind naturally extended itself to the household and frequenters of the palace, and became habitual even in the camp, combining itself curiously with the material restrictions of a military *régime*. Thus Heinrich Heine then sang, in a tone which recent German events still make but too familiar to European politics—

> Handle the drumstick and care not for life,
> Kiss, if you like her, the sutler's wife:
> That is the science worth discerning,
> That is the end of human learning.
> Drum every citizen out of his bed,
> Drum the *réveillé* into his head;

Preaching and drumming as long as you can,
That is the end of the life of man.
That is Philosophy *selon les règles,*
That is the doctrine according to Hegel:
I understand it, whoever may come,
For I am a capital hand at the drum.

The liberty too of religious speculation which Goethe has claimed as the ancestral privilege of the German mind,

For here each soul for freedom pants,
We are the natural Pròtèst-ants.

was still congenial to good society; and although in his later years the King had seemed inclined to measures of violence in the enforcement of a Lutheran state-religion, the latitude of opinion in the higher circles still savoured of the days and thoughts of Frederic the Great. For example, I remember great disgust being excited at some opera, in which there was a great deal of prayer represented on the stage—not with any reprehension of a supposed profanity, but as an exhibition of '*Pietismus.*' In such an atmosphere both Humboldt and Varnhagen von Ense could breathe freely, and associate agreeably even with men of reactionary politics and aristocratic prejudices. It will astonish many to read the

2

specimens of the intimate correspondence between Prince Metternich and a man whose political opinions he must have regarded as dangerous and detestable, but whose knowledge he could reverence, and of whose friendship he was proud.

With the reign of Frederic William IV. came a mode of thought and an estimate of men and things to which it was difficult, if not impossible, for the great minds which had battled through the glories and the ruins of the French Revolution to do justice. M. de Talleyrand used to say that only those who had lived near the conclusion of the last century could realise the worth of the world to man ; and we can fairly test the depth of those impressions by their endurance to the very last in the nobler spirits that had traversed the whole round of disappointment, and to whom all faith might well seem illusory and vain. 'In what condition do I leave the world,' writes Humboldt in 1853, 'I who remember 1789, and have shared in its emotions ? However, centuries are but seconds in the great process of the development of advancing humanity. Yet the rising curve has small bendings in it, and it is very inconvenient to find oneself on such a segment of its descending portion.' In the temper

of mind this sentence implies, neither Humboldt
nor Varnhagen could see anything but hypocrisy
or morbid sentiment in the religious medium
through which both philosophy and manners came
to be now regarded ; and in the prevalent fashion
of increased moral earnestness they could discern
little besides affectation, prejudice, and wilful
ignorance. When the audacious neologisms of
Bruno Bauer shocked the Court, Humboldt merely
wrote, 'Bruno has found me pre-Adamitically
converted; when I was young, the Court clergy
held opinions much the same as his. The minister
who confirmed me told me that the Evangelists
had made a variety of notes, out of which, in later
times, biographies had been poetically constructed.'

There can be no better illustration of the invincible repugnance of such men as these to the
intellectual tastes predominant in the King's
society, than their misapprehension of the character and opinions of Chevalier Bunsen. It was
natural enough that a somewhat arrogant aristocracy should resent the affectionate favour of the
King towards a self-made man of letters, and
should suspect him of designs dangerous to the
interests of their order, and involving social and
political change. But Humboldt and his corre-

spondent could not be affected by such motives;
indeed, the former was himself amenable to very
much the same accusations—so much so, that he
habitually absented himself from Court when the
Emperor Nicholas formed part of the circle, and
the King of Hanover so frankly expressed his contempt that he told him at his own table, 'that
there were two kind of animals always to be had
for money, to any amount—those that live by
their persons or their pens' (*Huren* and *Feder-
vieh*.)   It was mainly the Pietistic tendency in the
writings and supposed influences of Chevalier
Bunsen that made him an object almost of animosity to Varnhagen, who personally knew him little,
if at all, and of occasional unfriendly sarcasm to
Humboldt, who ought to have known him better.
The visit of the King of Prussia to England on
the occasion of the baptism of the Prince of
Wales was represented by these parties as an act
of prostration on the part of Prussia at the feet of
the British Tories, who certainly never troubled
their heads with any such fancies, and the mutual
arrangements for a Protestant bishopric of Jerusalem, as the enthronement of an Episcopal
Bench at Berlin, an ecclesiastical constitution which
assuredly has not resulted from that very harmless

proceeding. By a singular fatality Bunsen was
looked upon in this country with much suspicion
and ill-will, as a latitudinarian and neologist, while
he was abused and persecuted as an evangelical
fanatic on the banks of the Spree. If, in fact, a
theological sympathy may have been a bond of
union between him and his sovereign, and a step-
ping-stone towards his advancement in life, I know
of no instance where this interference led either of
the parties to injustice or to intolerance, which unfortunately cannot be said of the religious counsels
that prevailed in the later years of the monarch who
deserved a happier destiny. When the day of trial
came which was to determine whether Chevalier
Bunsen as a public man stood on the side of absolutism or constitutional liberty, of progress or of
reaction, he was not found wanting ; and, by sur-
rendering without hesitation the highest and most
lucrative post of his profession, and a residence which
had become to him a happy and a honoured home,
rather than subserve a policy which he deemed
unworthy of his country and injurious to mankind,
he dispersed the clouds of calumny and prejudice
which had so long obscured his name. Why did
he not live to see his most ambitious dreams of
German Unity more than realised, and the politi-

cians who treated him as an impracticable dreamer
the foremost actors on the scene ?

Humboldt himself could not have been an
active and earnest politician.   The largeness of his
views, derived from such long and accurate observations of nature and of men, must have induced
that indifference to the immediate contingencies of
human affairs which is at once the penalty and the
consolation of the highest and the fullest minds ;
otherwise it is difficult to conceive how he for so
many years endured the continual society of
public men whose principles and conduct he must
have regarded with animosity or disdain, and the
occurrence of daily events distressing to his feelings and repulsive to his judgment.   It was by
this abstinence that he probably retained an
influence which he could frequently exercise to
mitigate the severity of cases of individual oppres-
sion, and sometimes to sustain the really noble
and imaginative spirit of his royal master above
the sordid policy of expediency and of fear.   In
these efforts he scorned no assistance that offered
itself, not even that of the wilful, witty, and benevolent Bettina von Arnim, whom the King treated
with the same kind of admiring indulgence that
Goethe had done before him, allowing her to say

and write whatever she pleased, and, it may be, taking from her wayward wisdom advice that no graver counsellor would have dared to offer.

How grateful must have been the sympathetic expansion of unrestrained opinion with so congenial a mind as Varnhagen von Ense's to one who was but too conscious that he was looked upon by the society in which he lived as a sort of moral Helot —an example of what a man might come to, when drunk with knowledge ! No amount of diplomatic reserve could have made him acceptable to his fellow-courtiers, and it was only as a link between the intellectual qualities of the sovereign and the literature and science of the nation that he could feel himself in any legitimate vocation. In the various and remarkable creations of Art which have elaborately decorated the least lively of cities—in the great geographical and antiquarian explorations which Prussia has of late years undertaken, some of them in connection with English enterprise—in the composition and production of costly works of national or general interest—in the judicious and delicate relief of destitute men of letters, the authority of Humboldt was continuously and powerfully exercised without a suspicion of favouritism or partiality. Those who have had the good fortune to see him in the midst of that assembly of notable men whom the King of Prussia brings together on the festival of his 'Order of Merit,' will not forget with what ready reverence he was greeted by all—Poets, Historians, Painters, Sculptors, Geographers, Physicians, Philosophers, Professors of all arts and learning, as their intellectual chief, and how tranquilly he rested on his great reputation with the free and good will of all around.

Apart from these useful and honourable functions, the question may well be asked whether the connection of Baron Humboldt with the Court of Prussia was one which can be regarded with satisfaction relatively to the dignity of literature and the worth of the human mind. And yet, if not this, what position of any man of genius or the highest erudition in the constant intimacy of any court is desirable or even tenable? Enjoying the entire esteem and real friendship of two sovereigns, one of them a man of grave intelligence, proved by many severe vicissitudes of fortune and a foremost figure in the catastrophes of modern Europe, the other a most pleasant and accomplished gentleman, full of generous impulses, and only deficient in the sterner purpose and more explicit will that his times required, Humboldt remains as unindulgent to the princely character as if he were an outer democrat, and falls foul even of our amiable and intellectual Prince Consort, who approached him with a cordial admiration which would have been very acceptable to any English man of letters. What Philosopher at Court can be expected to keep his judgment clear and his temper cool where the wise and kindly Humboldt so failed?

The wide gulf which in our country separates the men of thought from the men of action is assuredly no small evil. In its effect on the political and social character of the upper ranks it maintains a low standard of mental labour, content with official aptitude, with adroit representation, and with facility of speech, and disparages the exercise of those spontaneous and constructive faculties which should also give a man the command of his fellows in a reflective age; it encourages the consumption of a large portion of life in amusements which become occupations, serious frivolities only differing from vices as barren ground differs from weeds, and really perilous to the moral peace of the community, by contrasting the continuous task of the working

2*

thousand with the incessant pleasure of the selected few. On the other hand, the isolation of the literary class has not only deformed some of our highest works of fiction by caricatures of manners and motives with which the writers have not been sufficiently familiar, but has also engendered a sense of injustice which shows itself in wrong susceptibilities, in idle vaunts, in uncharitable interpretations, and in angry irony. These painful feelings may rather increase than diminish with the practical equality that is advancing upon us with such rapid strides (but which the literary class are so often unwilling themselves to concede to others), and the imagined barrier may be all the more formidable when it ceases to rest on the palpable inequalities of fortune and the real dissimilarity of daily existence.

Let, however, no displeasure at the separation or even hostilities of the two superiorities, either here or elsewhere, blind us to the paramount importance of the independence of the literary character. So noble, indeed, was the nature of Alexander von Humboldt, that it preserved, under an almost life-long weight of patronage, the elevation of his intellect and the integrity of his heart. His indefatigable industry was unimpeded by the

constant round of small duties and vapid amusements, and the luxurious security of his official
position never blunted his eager interest in the
new acquisitions of all science, and in the fresh
developments of literature. It was thus his signal
good fortune to retain to the last, not only the
wonderful stores of knowledge accumulated
through so many years, but also the art to reproduce and dispose them for the delight and edifica-
tion of mankind. Some affectation in demeanour
and expression was the inevitable consequence of
a factitious mode of life, but we would attribute
much of the hyperbolic tone that pervades a portion
of his correspondence to the traditional habits of a
former generation, when adulation was polite and
the best friends were ceremonious, rather than to
any infection of disingenuous manners. So
notable an exception to ordinary rules and expectations as the career of Humboldt, should assuredly check the desire that those who occupy
' the heights and pinnacles of human mind ' should
be exposed to similar temptations. No advantage,
however great, should be purchased at so costly a
price as the sacrifice of that which is the only sure
sign of the progress of nations, and the very core
of civilization itself, the combination of moral

strength with intellectual culture. There is thus
something satisfactory in Humboldt's very dissatisfaction, in his criticism of the great, in his consciousness of an incomplete and jarring existence,
in his struggle to escape from a conventional world
to the confidences of a genial and undoubted
friendship. Without these emotions, without this
generous discontent, all the learning and all the wit
of the companion in letters and mental counsellor
of Frederic William, might not have saved him
from the servility and its consequences which degraded the incensor of Frederic the Great—'M.
de Voltaire, Gentilhomme du Roi,'—and from a
relation to his accomplished master not without
some analogy to that which in ruder times was
occupied by the Professor of the Cap and Bells.

III.

CARDINAL WISEMAN.

In the winter of 1830–31 the British Catholics were represented at Rome by Cardinal Weld, of the Welds of Lulworth Castle. His Eminence was an English country-gentleman, of the simplest manners, of no literary pretensions, of liberal politics, as were indeed all his Catholic countrymen in those days, and delighting to do the honours of the Eternal City to persons in any way connected with his family and home. It was to an intimacy of this kind that I was indebted for my introduction to the *Collegio Inglese*, at that time presided over by Dr. Wiseman. Among the students under his care was a young cousin of the name of Macarthy, with whom I soon formed a lasting friendship, and thus I was brought into frequent relations with the rector of the College. These two men, Cardinal Wiseman, Catholic Archbishop of Westminster, and Sir Charles Macarthy, Governor of Ceylon, passed away within a few months of each other,

the younger going first; each having done, in his
separate walk of life, that which is a man's first
duty—to use the talents given to his charge for
what he believes to be a right purpose, and
honestly to win the respect and regard of mankind.

There was then in the English College the fresh
recollection of the grateful jubilee that had been
held to celebrate the political emancipation of the
Catholics of Great Britain by the long efforts and
frequent sacrifices of the Liberal party in Parliament; and Dr. Wiseman was looked upon with
little good-will by those who were content to base
the spiritual and temporal government of the world
on a relation of absolute authority and obedience.
He had withdrawn his pupils from their attendance
on the lectures at the Jesuit College; and it was
rumoured that Pope Gregory XVI. had by no
means maintained the amicable feelings which had
been manifested towards him by Pope Leo XII., his
fast friend and patron.   However that might be, Dr.
Wiseman pursued an independent course of action,
and impressed on all who came within the more
intimate circle of his acquaintance his sincere desire
to reconcile the liberties of literature and science
with a respectful recognition of his ecclesiastical
position.

His life and education had been somewhat cosmopolitan. Some German translator of his ' Horæ Syriacæ ' had described him in one many-syllabled word as the ' from-an-Irish-family-descended-in-Spain-born-in-England-educated-in-Italy-consecrated Syrian scholar,' but he showed no inclination to merge his British nationality in his sacerdotal or scholastic character. His conversation ran mainly on subjects of English literature, and his greatest pleasure was to converse with his intellectual fellow-countrymen. He encouraged those tastes and habits among his pupils, as far as was consistent with the practices of a Catholic seminary. The books which were read aloud, according to conventual custom, during the noontide repast, were usually our British classics; and I remember, on more than one occasion of this kind, listening to a novel of Walter Scott's. Dr. Cullen was at that time the rector of the Irish College; but although I have met the future Catholic Primate of Ireland on high-days in the hall of the *Collegio Inglese*, there was little intercourse between the two establishments, and apparently no close intimacy between the heads. The two bodies always walked separately in processions at great church ceremonies; and I am not aware that any of my

English fellow-countrymen ever received such a
tribute of fervid admiration as was paid to their
Irish comrades while, in their due turn, they were
bearing aloft the Holy Father through the colon-
nades of St. Peter's at the Festival of Corpus
Christi, when a young English lady, having exclaimed, ' Oh, papa ! do look at those handsome
young priests ; did you ever see such fine eyes ? '
was dreadfully shocked by the answer of one of
them in an unmistakable accent—' Thank you,
Miss, for the compliment.'

Another Irish ecclesiastic, however—Dr. McHale,
then Bishop of Killala—seemed more familiar with
the inmates of the *Collegio Inglese ;* perhaps from
the very contrast of his character to that of the
scholarly and courteous Dr. Wiseman, who used to
watch the various demonstrations of his Hibernian
zeal with considerable interest and amusement.
That persistent nationality—which during his long
career as Archbishop of Tuam has not only alienated Dr. McHale from all social intercourse with
the representatives of British power in Ireland, but
which has caused him to include in one sweeping
denunciation the fiercest acts of old oppressors
and the most benevolent efforts of modern legis-
lators—the ' thorough ' Strafford and the gentle

Carlisle—has remained unaffected by the passive political attitude which it has always been the habit of the Roman Court to assume in Irish affairs, and refused to surrender an iota of his rights of resistance to any civil authority. It is only just to Archbishop McHale to say that he has maintained during the late General Council the same independent attitude towards the Papal Curia, and was foremost in such opposition, as ecclesiastical decorum permitted, to the obnoxious doctrine. But in 1831 the example of Poland, just then succumbing after an heroic struggle to the colossus of the North, not only without the active sympathy of the Papal power but with the distinct injunction to her ecclesiastics to submit humbly to the schismatic conqueror, was not calculated to assure or appease the spirit of the Celtic prelate, who might have anticipated a period when British diplomacy might turn against the Irish Catholic Church even her own spiritual arms, and coerce her to obedience by ultramontane aid—a result at that time by no means improbable ; for who then dreamt of the political destiny of Italy, which was quietly approaching to its dawn ? Who then cared to trouble the pleasant somnolence of Art and Antiquity, in which the Princes and Peoples between the Alps and the sea reposed, with

any more serious agitation than a commentary on
Dante, the merits of Santa Filomèna, or the respective claims of the mature Pasta and the youthful Grisi ?   Happy days those for the tourist, whom
no one troubled about his opinions or his religion—
for the archæologist, who looked on Italy as an
inexhaustible necropolis, and found it so—and for
the collector, to whom every day noble poverty
surrendered treasures of art and curiosities of history at a moderate cost, with *giallo antico* not exhausted and constitutions undiscovered !

Yet, although the Protestant visitors of the
English College were perfectly secure from any
intrusive proselytism, and the only influences of the
kind brought to bear were fair controversy when
challenged and amiable inducements to see all that
was best and most striking in the practice and
symbolic action of the Roman Church, there was
no concealment of the special interest attached to
the circumstances and conduct of recent British
converts.   A Cornish baronet, far advanced in life,
had not only professed himself a Roman Catholic,
but, at his urgent desire, had been ordained a
priest.*   The deepest anxiety was expressed as to

* Sir Harry Trelawney, grandfather of the present consistent Liberal member for East Cornwall.

his first performance of his mystical office, and it was hinted that a more than natural power of retentive memory was vouchsafed to him on the occasion. The son of Earl Spencer, who afterwards became notorious as Brother Ignatius, was at that time a resident in the College, and his first sermon in the church set apart for the service of the English Catholics excited an intense interest among the students ; and here, too, the success, though not very apparent to us curious Protestants, was a subject of much thankfulness. In all such matters Dr. Wiseman's interest was always affectionate and judicious, and never provoked any sense of extravagance in the outsiders.

Soon after the French Revolution of 1830 a remarkable company of Frenchmen arrived at Rome. The Abbé Lamennais, whose previous and future career I may assume to be generally known, came to demand justice of the Chair of St. Peter against the throne of the *bourgeois* Gallican king. His enterprise of opening the public education of France to the free competition of the Church had been arrested by the law ; and his young colleague, the Comte de Montalembert, had just commenced his strange and varied public life of distracted opinion and irreconcilable tendencies, which has lately closed amid the affectionate sympathies and just recognition of the two countries he loved with an equal filial duty, by an eloquent and fruitless defence of the cause at the bar of the *Chambre des Pairs.* These two remarkable men were accompanied by the Abbé Lacordaire, the future successor of Bossuet and Massillon, and by M. Rio, now well known throughout Europe as the graceful and pious historian of Christian Art. Lamennais, like Dr. Wiseman, had received Pope Leo XII.'s intellectual sympathy and honourable protection, and the author of the ' Essai sur l'Indifférence' was known to have been designated at that time for the highest dignities of the Church ; but another spirit now predominated in the Roman Court, and he and his lieutenants were received with more than coldness and disregard. It did not, perhaps, become any non-Catholic to judge the causes of this policy, yet it certainly appeared to the casual observer that the dominant motives of the actors in these scenes were the disinclination to quarrel with the representatives of a successful revolution in France, and an indistinct dread of the large and popular basis on which the Abbé Lamennais was content to rest the authority and destiny of the Catholic Church. It is, however, no

doubt open for any believer to discern in this repudiation of the future heretic and revolutionist a
superior prescience of the danger of giving trust
or favor to a lofty intelligence liable to serious aber-
ration, and a mind too haughty to be steadfast in
its service to any external rule. Be this as it
may, the immediate impression was eminently disagreeable. You saw a man who had grown great
in the defence of the Church, now that he had
pushed forward some theories, which had the acceptance of the more earnest Catholics in France,
with an inconvenient enthusiasm, not only left unsupported in his struggle but regarded with aver-
sion. He had difficulty in even getting access to
the Pope; and one day, when he showed some
little resentment on this score, a Monsignore su-
perciliously observed that the Abbé surely did not
come from a country in which his order were
treated with especial respect. 'You are mistaken,
sir,' said Lamennais; 'in France no one despises
a priest—they reverence him, or they kill him,'—a
remark singularly corroborated by the successive
violent deaths of three Archbishops of Paris.

To these missionaries of a wider and braver
Catholicism Dr. Wiseman proffered a generous
hospitality, which was thankfully received. The

minute person and phthisical constitution of Lamennais did not permit him to take any important part
in general society; but the charm and earnestness
of Montalembert—so French in his emotions and
so English in his thoughts—competed with the
simple, audacious spontaneity of his Breton colleague Rio—a Christian in politics and an Artist in
religion—to make the conversation of the decorous
Seminary as bright and coloured as that of the
gayest Paris drawing-room. After the publication
of the ' Affaires de Rome' the breach between the
Abbé Lamennais and the Church probably precluded all future intercourse between the reformer
and the prelate: the host of that table rose in
honourable gradation to the loftiest functions of his
profession; and of the guest I will only record
what a French artisan said to me in 1848, when I
asked whether he knew by chance where M.
Lamennais lodged?—' Dans cette maison-là très-
haute—tout près du ciel.'

This is not the place to praise or criticise the
lectures on the ' Connection between Science and
Revealed Religion,' which I heard delivered by
Dr. Wiseman in the apartments of Cardinal Weld
during the Lent of 1835. But it is well to remember that at that time the subject was compara-

tively new, and the knowledge imparted in a great
degree necessarily derived from original sources.
The matter was not then contained in popular
works, but had to be sought at first-hand.   As the
teleological arguments which the Bridgewater
Treatises and their successors have urged to weari-
ness had not then familiarised the public mind with
the connection between the truths of Science and
those of Natural Religion, so the abundant illustrations which Scripture may derive from ethnology,
philology, and archæology were then confined to
the learned, and had not been made the staple of
endless lectures, essays, and dictionaries.   Thus
these discourses were most interesting to all who
heard them, and though, perhaps, the wide range
they took created some distrust in the perfect
accuracy of the author, yet his acknowledged eminence in one portion of Oriental philology fairly
suggested the inference that he would not run the
risk of careless assertions or inadequate knowledge
in other portions of his work.   He did not give
these lectures to the public till after his settlement
in England, and even then with some hesitation, as
the preface avers.   In announcing the publication
to myself, he wrote: 'In a moment of great
presumption I resolved to premise to them a sonnet

by way of dedication.   I send it for your friendly
inspection, requesting not merely that you will
suggest any alteration, but that you will frankly
say, if you think so, that it will not do.   For I am
far from believing myself anything so great as a
poet.'   This was the sonnet :—

> Some dive for pearls to crown a mortal brow,
> Some fondly garlands weave to dress the shrine
> Of fading beauty : so is my design,
> Learning t'enchase that lay concealed till now,
> And from known science pluck each greenest bough ;
> But not to deck the earthly, while divine
> Beauty and majesty, supreme as thine,
> Religion ! shall my humble gift allow.
> Thine was my childhood's path-lamp, and the oil
> Of later watchings hath but fed the flame
> While I, embroid'ring here with pleasant toil
> My imaged traceries around thy name,
> This banner weave, in part from hostile spoil,
> And pay my fealty to thy highest claim.

In a postscript he added, 'Even if approved, I
do not think that I shall have courage to publish
it.'   The friend thus appealed to may probably
have suggested that the lectures would be quite as
well without the ' verses dedicatory ; ' and I am not
aware that they have ever appeared in print; but
they are now not without a touching interest of
their own, not only from the becoming diffidence

shown by a man who even then lived among much
to encourage vanity and self-confidence, but from
the simple sentiment they express, and which his
whole life illustrated. It has been stated that,
shortly before his death, the Cardinal assembled
the Chapter of his church around his bed, and
expressed to them his thankfulness that he had
never been troubled by any difficulties or mental
anxiety in matters of faith. These lectures convey precisely that impression. If science can
make itself useful and ancillary to faith, so much
the better for science. As Lamennais himself
once wrote, 'Le monde matériel est Dieu mis en
doute : gare à celui qui se laisse prendre !'

It was with no intention of leading a secluded
or scholastic life that Dr. Wiseman came to England. He mixed freely in the interests and topics
of the time, and I have just laid my hand on a
letter in which he describes his attendance at a
great meeting for the Irish Protestant clergy.
'Heartily,' he writes, 'as I pity the individuals in
distress, and wish that the triumph which is achiev-
ing could be bought without inflicting the slightest
suffering on any human being, the tales which were
unfolded could not but excite in my mind a feeling
of self-congratulation and joy in thinking that I

8

was, perhaps, the only one in that assembled multitude who saw therein a stroke of retributive justice for injuries long inflicted under the pretence of religion. I have just come from Ireland, remember, from my first visit after twenty-five years, and I have warmed my patriotism at my domestic hearth, in the hall of my forefathers, who suffered and died for their religion. But I am getting into Mr. M——'s vein—*alias* King Cambyses'. Mr. M—— was one of the speakers, and certainly very eloquent, but ranting and scenic.'

Both at Oscott, where he superintended a college founded in a wholesome spirit of rivalry to the monopoly of Stonyhurst in the education of the Catholic gentry of England, and in his offices of Coadjutor and of Bishop of the London District, Dr. Wiseman extended his society beyond his co-religionists, and would in time have come to be regarded as any other distinguished man of letters. A decorous precedence was willingly given to him in Protestant houses, and he was becoming gradually esteemed as an author, although naturally his books were received with more favour and less criticism among those who sympathised with his opinions and objects than by the general reader. His style never became agreeable to ordinary

English taste ; the foreign education of his young manhood damaged the force and even the correctness of his diction, and a certain natural taste for richness of form and colour encumbered his writings with superfluous epithets and imagery. These defects would no doubt have been diminished by a longer and more frequent intercourse with the best instructed of his countrymen ; but in the year 1850 he returned to Rome, with the intention, it was reported, of taking up his abode there. I remember indeed his saying to his cousin Macarthy, who was then rising fast towards the highest grades of the Colonial Service, 'When you are tired of governing in all parts of the world, come and visit me in my *terzo piano* of —— ' some Roman palace which he particularly liked—I think it was the 'Colonna.' But no such repose was in store for him. He returned to England, the first Roman Cardinal that had stood on British soil since Pole had died amid the fires of Smithfield, with the missive from the Flaminian gate in his hand, the agent of a bloodless but not innocuous revolution.

The story of the so-called Papal Aggression has yet to be written. The circumstances of the affair were crowded with misapprehension on all sides. There had been much to induce the belief,

on the part of the Catholics, that a Prince of the
Roman Church and Court would be received without disfavour in England.   The Government had
only lately passed an Act of Parliament author-
ising diplomatic relations with Rome ; and in the
debate on Lord Eglintoun's clause, which limited
the selection of the Papal envoys to this country
to laymen, it had been distinctly stated in the
House of Lords, on the Liberal side, that there
would be no objection to the presence of a
Cardinal in England.   Again, the extent and
power of the High Church party that had lately
developed itself at Oxford was extravagantly
exaggerated by the Catholics, both at home and
at Rome.   The entirely intellectual character of
the movement, and the certainty of its indignant
repulse the moment it came into contact with the
habits, instincts, and traditions of the English
people, were not perceptible to Dr. Wiseman,
whose recent few years of residence in his native
land could not compensate for an early life of
foreign impressions.   How far he may have been
encouraged in his notion of the improved feelings
of this country toward Roman Catholicism by
members of the Tractarian party I have no means
of knowing ; but with some of them he had

friendly relations, and he had been one of the first of the authorities of his Church to approach them with a sympathetic interest, and to attract them to what he believed the only safe conclusion by a kindly appreciation of their doubts and difficulties.

He had also had an interview and conversation with Lord John Russell before he left England for Italy, of which he always spoke as affording a vindication of his future proceedings. Its confidential and private nature, he said, prevented him from appealing to it during his lifetime; but he had written a record of it, which must, some day, be generally known, and would seriously affect the estimate of the imprudence of his conduct. If this is so, it is the more singular that the first overt act declaratory of opinion in high places, and premonitory of public indignation, should have proceeded from Lord John Russell. What was called the 'Durham letter' was no doubt his personal production, and in no way sanctioned by his Cabinet; but it had all the effect of a political encyclic. Looking back on the affair, after the lapse of years, the chief mistake seems to have been the simultaneity of the new ecclesiastical arrangement and the advent of the Cardinal Archbishop. Either the one or the other by itself would have met with the usual amount of popular criticism as an unwelcome novelty, and have died away after a nine-days' bluster. When the vivacity of public feeling then aroused is remembered, it now seems fortunate for the religious liberties of our country that the issue was no worse than the Ecclesiastical Titles Bill, which in its result, and probably in the intent, exactly corresponded with the judgment of an *abus de pouvoir* delivered by the French High Court against the prelates who interfere too prominently in political concerns. It was an official censure, *quantum valeat*, and nothing more. An eminent foreign statesman said to me that if we had civilly conducted him to Dover with an escort, and put him on board a ship, we should have acted in strict accordance with the traditions of Catholic Governments.

But on the minds of individual Catholics, especially those prominently engaged in the matter, the Protestant demonstration produced a sense of indignant surprise. There was so much to be said in their favour on logical grounds, and the inferences from arguments of religious freedom were so patent, that the public condemnation struck them as something beyond the ordinary condition of public policy, and as tainted with personal ill-feeling and special injustice. Thus the Cardinal placed himself before his countrymen in the attitude of constant reproach for a grave wrong committed not only against his person and his community, but against the liberal principles of the men and the party with whom the Catholics of England had been for so long connected. His position among us must, in any case, have been somewhat anomalous and discomfortable. The social rank of the Cardinalate had frequently formed the subject of dispute with half the Courts of Christendom. It had been asserted to be higher than that of the members of the Royal Family itself in any foreign country, inasmuch as every Cardinal was not only a prince of the Roman State, but *particeps regni Romani*, and as such notified his accession to all Catholic sovereigns. And though this assumption has been rarely, if ever, admitted, yet it is difficult to imagine where that awful tribunal the 'Board of Green Cloth' could have decided to range the Cardinal, so as to be agreeable to the feelings of the Papal Court, and even to the custom of Catholic countries, and not to shock the precise and historical gradations of rank assigned to the subjects of the British Crown. He had, indeed, himself so little anticipated any difficulty on this score, that he brought over with him the curious mediæval trappings of the horses that drew the cardinals' carriages in Rome on state occasions; yet it turned out that even in the various circles of private life the Cardinal was much restricted by the dignity of his position. He had to be treated as a Prince in a society which dislikes ostentation and restraint, and which becomes exclusive from its inclination to ease and equality. He did not fare better in his individual relations with the Protestant world; they gradually became weaker even where they had been the closest; and, except on such occasions as his appearance as a lecturer at the Royal Institution, his last years were passed in the diligent discharge of his episcopal duties, and in company where his intellectual as well as his social superiority remained unchallenged.

Apart from the advantages which the internal administration of the Roman Catholic Church in this country may have derived from the change, it now appears very questionable whether the coming of Cardinal Wiseman is not rather a subject of regret than of happy retrospect to the Catholics themselves. It began by driving out of public life for the time some most estimable men, such as the late Duke of Norfolk and Mr. Torrens M'Cullagh, who led the hopeless opposition to the Ecclesiastical Titles Bill; it made it next to impossible, for many years to come, for any Catholic to represent an English constituency; it embittered the fair discussion of questions in which the discipline and the customs of the Roman Catholic Church come into contact either with the moral prejudices or the intellectual pretensions of their Protestant fellow-countrymen; it reopened the ancient wounds of Irish party animosity which the great common calamity of the famine had gone far to cauterise; it dissociated the leading Catholics in England from those liberal traditions which, if unbroken, might now enable them to do a signal service to their age and their religion, by making them the mediators between the providential necessities of the fruitful present and the deep-rooted associations of decaying systems. And now it has passed away from the statute-book almost without notice, except from the curious fact that it was the prelates of the Protestant Church of Ireland who became, after their disestablismment, mainly obnoxious to its provisions.

3*

There was a large field of ecclesiastical usefulness open to Nicholas Wiseman, had not circumstances, rather than conduct, placed him in a groove in which he was compelled to continue to the end. The supposition which I have heard expressed, even by the Roman Catholic clergy, that he might have ascended the chair of St. Peter, after the demise of its present occupant, is extravagant. The Italian portion of the Conclave, as long at least as any temporal power is throned in the Vatican, will not relax the rule, established centuries ago, to limit the selection of the Pope to the *prelatura* of Italy ; nor is it probable that there would be ever such a concordance of opinion in the representatives of other nations as to afford any chance of breaking down this monopoly. But even though he had never attained any of the highest clerical dignities, Dr. Wiseman, in the ordinary course of his profession, would have exercised a very wide moral influence by the general justice of his mind and the sweetness of his disposition. If he had to be intolerant, it was against the grain ; and perhaps he gladly took refuge in a somewhat pompous rhetoric from the necessity of plainly expressing unpalatable truths and harsh conclusions. Such at least is the estimate of one who knew him intimately for many years, and who will ever retain a pleasant and affectionate memory of his talents and his virtues.

WALTER SAVAGE LANDOR.

IV.

WALTER SAVAGE LANDOR.

THERE were few visitors to Florence between
the years 1829 and 1835 whose attention had not
in some way been directed to an elderly English
gentleman, residing with his family in a commodious villa on the pleasant slope of those Fiesolan
hills, full of the scenes and memories of history
—with the cottage of Dante, the palace of
Michael Angelo, and the home of Machiavelli in
sight, and overlooking the Valarno and Vallombrosa which Milton saw and sang. He had lived
previously for six years in the city, at the Palazzo
Medici, and for a short time in another *campagna*,
but had few acquaintances among his countrymen
except artists, and scarcely any among the natives
except picture-dealers. He had a stately and
agreeable presence, and the men-of-letters from
different countries who brought introductions to
him spoke of his affectionate reception, of his

WALTER SAVAGE LANDOR.

IV.

WALTER SAVAGE LANDOR.

THERE were few visitors to Florence between
the years 1829 and 1835 whose attention had not
in some way been directed to an elderly English
gentleman, residing with his family in a commodious villa on the pleasant slope of those Fiesolan
hills, full of the scenes and memories of Boccaccio
—with the cottage of Dante, the birthplace of
Michael Angelo, and the home of Machiavelli in
sight, and overlooking the Valdarno and Vallombrosa which Milton saw and sang. He had lived
previously for six years in the city, at the Palazzo
Medici, and for a short time in another *campagna*,
but had few acquaintances among his countrymen
except artists, and scarcely any among the natives
except picture-dealers. He had a stately and
agreeable presence, and the men-of-letters from
different countries who brought introductions to
him spoke of his affectionate reception, of his com-

plimentary old-world manners, and his elegant though simple hospitality. But it was his conversation that left on them the most delightful and permanent impression ; so affluent, animated, and coloured, so rich in knowledge and illustration, so gay and yet so weighty—such bitter irony and such lofty praise, uttered with a voice fibrous in all its tones, whether gentle or fierce—it equalled, if not surpassed, all that has been related of the table-talk of men eminent for social speech. It proceeded from a mind so glad of its own exercise, and so joyous in its own humour, that in its most extravagant notions and most exaggerated attitudes it made argument difficult and criticism superfluous. And when memory and fancy were alike exhausted, there came a laughter so pantomimic, yet so genial, rising out of a momentary silence into peals so cumulative and sonorous, that all contradiction and possible affront were merged for ever.

This was the author of the ' Imaginary Conversations,' who was esteemed by many high authorities in our own and in classical literature to be the greatest living master of the Latin and English tongues. But it was not the speaker, real or fictitious, or the writer, less or more meritorious, who had made so wide a repute in that flowery town, not yet conscious of the burdens and honours of patriotism, but sufficiently happy in its beauty and its insignificance. His notoriety referred to a supposed eccentricity of conduct and violence of demeanour that exceeded the licence which our countrymen, by no means original at home, are believed to claim and require when travelling or resident abroad. The strange notions and peculiar form of these ebullitions had woven themselves into a sort of legend. It was generally accepted that he had been sent away from school after thrashing the Head-master, who had ventured to differ from him as to the quantity of a syllable in a Latin verse; that he had been expelled from the University after shooting at a Fellow of a College, who took the liberty of closing a window to exclude the noise of his wine party; that he had been outlawed from England for felling to the ground a barrister who had had the audacity to subject him to a cross-examination. His career on the Continent bore an epical completeness. The poet Monti having written a sonnet adulatory of Napoleon and offensive to England, Mr. Landor replied in such outspoken Latinity that he was summoned by the authorities of Como to answer to the charge of libel ; he proceeded to threaten the *Regio Delegato* with a *bella bastonata,* and avoided being conducted to Milan by a voluntary retirement to Genoa, launching a Parthian epigram at Count Strasoldo, the Austrian Governor, still more opprobious than the former verse. At Florence he had been frequently on the point of expulsion, and could expect little protection from the English Embassy, having challenged the Secretary of the Legation for whistling in the street when Mrs. Landor passed, and having complained to the Foreign Office of ' the wretches it employed abroad.' Once he was positively banished and sent to Lucca,—the legend ran, for walking up a Court of Justice, where the Judges were hearing a complaint he had made against an Italian servant, with a bag of dollars in his hand, and asking how much was necessary to secure a favourable verdict, —' not for his own sake, but for the protection of his countrymen in the city.' Either in deprecation of this sentence, or in the consolation of the thought that he only shared the fate of the great Poet and Exile of Florence, he wrote—

Oro

Ne, Florentia, me voces poetam :
Nam collem peragrare Fæsulanum,
Jucundum est mihi—nec lubenter hortos

Fontesque, aut nemorum algidos recessus,
Primo invisere mane vesperique
Exul desinerem: exulatque quisquis,
O Florentia ! dixeris poetam.

At the time, however, to which we have alluded, he was living in more than ordinary tranquillity, and having vented his rage against all kings and constituted authorities in his writings, he submitted with common decorum to the ordinances of government and society. But the demon of discord was too strong within him, and ere a few years had lapsed, he was once more in England, but more than ever an exile, having left behind the home of his choice, the young family of his caresses, the pictures he had domesticated, the nature that had grown a familiar friend. And by a strange relentlessness of destiny, he was at last driven forth once more, back to a home that had become homeless, to an alienated household, to a land that had for him no longer any flowers but to grow over his grave.

Mr. Forster, in his interesting volumes, has added to the tragic biographies of men of genius— of Otway and of Savage, of Byron and of Keats. He has performed a task, which his reverent friendship of many years made most difficult and delicate, with dignity and affection. Nothing is concealed that is worth revealing, nothing is

lauded which is unjust, and nothing is left unre-
proved and unregretted which is wrong in moral
conception or unbecoming in the action of life. In
this conduct of his subject he has followed the
dictates of the highest prudence ; he has shown that
if the temperament of his friend made him most
troublesome to the societies in which he lived,
made his acquaintance uneasy and his friendship
perilous, it was he himself who was the foremost
sufferer ; that neither honourable birth, nor independent fortune, nor sturdy health, nor a marriage
of free choice, nor a goodly family, nor rare talents,
nor fine tastes, nor appropriate culture, nor sufficient fame, could ensure him a life of even
moderate happiness, while the events of the day
depended on the wild instincts of the moment,
while the undisciplined and thoughtless will over-
ruled all capacity of reflection and all suggestions
of experience. Not but that many wilful and
impatient men enjoy their domestic tyranny, and
make a good figure in public life, and possibly owe
much of their pleasure and success to the very
annoyance they inflict. ' I should have been nowhere without my temper,' said an uncomfortable
politician of the last generation, and those who
knew him best agreed with him. But in Landor's

idiosyncrasy there were but two men, conscious of each other's acts and feelings. By the side of, or rather above, the impulsive, reckless creature, there was the critical, humorous, nature, as well aware of its own defect as any enemy could be, ever strong enough to show and probe the wound, but impotent to heal it, and pathetically striving to remedy, through the judgments of the intellect, the faults and the miseries of the living actor. Thus nowhere in the range of the English language are the glory and happiness of moderation of mind more nobly preached and powerfully illustrated than in the writings of this most intemperate man; nowhere is the sacredness of the placid life more hallowed and honoured than in the utterances of this tossed and troubled spirit; nowhere are heroism and self-sacrifice and forgiveness more eloquently adored than by this intense and fierce individuality, which seemed unable to forget for an instant its own claims, its own wrongs, its own fancied superiority over all its fellow-men.

I am conscious that in mingling my reminiscences with the details of this memoir, I am mainly consulting my own satisfaction; yet it may be that I shall give some enjoyment to a scholarly circle, to men who value culture for its own sake, who care for the appropriate quotation and love the ring of the epigram, who take a pleasure in style analogous to that derived from a musical perception, to whom beautiful thoughts come with tenfold meaning when beautifully said; a class visibly narrowing about us, but to whom, nevertheless, this country has owed a large amount of rational happiness, and whom the aspirants after a more rugged and sincere intellectual life may themselves not be the last to regret.

Landor was proud of a good descent: he wrote, and would often say, 'To be well-born is the greatest of all God's primary blessings, and there are many well-born among the poor and needy.' He was of an old Staffordshire race, said to be originally, 'De la Laundes,' united, in the person of his mother, with that of the Savages of Warwickshire, from whom he inherited the estate of Ipsley Court and Tachbrooke (the Tacæa, 'brightest-eyed of Avon's train,' of his tender farewell song); while a smaller property in Buckinghamshire, now in the possession of the first professed man-of-letters who has risen to be Prime Minister of this country, passed to younger children. The boy went to Rugby School at the usual age; and there began that magnetic attraction to Classical

Literature which grew till he was incorporated with it as his mental self. The Head-master—repelled or troubled by his peculiar nature, so self-contained at that early age that he never would compete with anyone for anything, but stood upon the work's worth, whatever it might be,—with so nice sense of justice, that he paid his fag for all service that he rendered him—took neither sufficient pride nor interest to conciliate the better or subdue the worse within him. Thus after some years they quarrelled —truly, and according to the legend, about the quantity of a syllable, in which Landor was right; not, however, so far as to come to blows, but to words that made reconciliation impossible. Might not a more appreciative and affectionate supervision have done something to arrest the first growths of this untoward temper, and have better accommodated it to the exigencies of coming life? Surely some such notion must have come across Landor's own mind when, long after, he 'happened to think on poor James,' and wrote, 'before I went to sleep'—

--------hostis olim tu mihi tibique ego,
Qui meque teque jam videntes crederent?
Ah! cur reductis abnuebas naribus
Spectans refrigeransque lævo lumine,
Cui primum amicus ingenuusque omnis puer
Et cui secundum esse ipse æmulus daret locum?

Sed hanc habebis, hanc habebo, gratiam,
Quum carmine istorum excidas, vives meo.

Nor again at Oxford, where he entered Trinity College at eighteen years of age, in the memorable year of 1793, did he find any head or heart strong enough to guide him. He wrote better Latin verses than any undergraduate or graduate in the University ; but no one cared for, or indeed saw, them except a Rugby schoolmate, Walter Birch, a cultivated Tory parson, who remained his friend through life, and Cary, the future translator of Dante. Outside of Oxford, he had already made the acquaintance, at Warwick, of a great scholar, who seems to us to have had more influence over his life and character, and not wholly in a favourable sense, than any other man—Dr. Parr. In the two men there was a close similarity, not only of taste, but of disposition ; it was certainly happy for the confirmation of Landor in his peculiar work as a representative of English scholarship, that he found in Parr a congenial intelligence of the highest order of accomplishment ; but it was not equally well for him to have continually before him, in the person he most venerated, the example of a temperament almost as wilful and as insolent as his own. Taking from Dr. Johnson the tradition of evincing independence of thought by roughness of manner, and of masking a kindly temperament under a rude and sometimes malicious exterior, Dr. Parr encouraged and vindicated the peculiarities of his younger disciple. The fierce pleasantry with which Parr flogged the boys the oftenest he liked the best and from whom he expected the most, had no analogy in Landor's disposition, which had an instinctive horror of cruelty of all kinds; and it is curious to find him sending from Oxford to the sanguinary schoolmaster a small disquisition on the doctrine of the Metempsychosis, which he conceived Pythagoras to have invented to induce savage natures to be humane even to birds and insects for their own sakes, inasmuch as their turn might come when they assumed similar forms of life. This paper contained besides some other matter, which he conceived Coleridge to have appropriated, and to which he, many years afterwards, grandly alluded as 'estrays and waifs not worth claiming by the Lord of the Manor. Coleridge and Wordsworth are heartily welcome to a day's sport over any of my woodlands and heaths. I have no preserves.'

In the youthful sports of either place he took no interest. At Rugby, fishing had pleased him by its solitude, and he would say he remembered liking sculling on the Isis, ' mainly because he could not swim, which gave an excitement to the exercise.' He soon earned the then abhorred reputation of a Jacobin. The assumed ferocity which made him in later life describe Robespierre as ' having some sins of commission to answer for—more of omission,' and tell Mr. Willis, the American, that ' he kept a purse of a hundred sovereigns ready for any one that should rid the world of a tyrant, not excepting an American President,' had a more practical meaning at the time when the approval of the French republic was a contemporaneous opinion, manifesting itself in such patent acts as wearing his hair unpowdered and queue tied with black ribbon—enormities only exceeded by that of a student of Balliol, who had gone into Hall in flowing locks, of the name of Robert Southey. Strange that these partners in rebellion, destined to the closest and longest of friendships, there never met—Southey afterwards writing that ' he would have sought his acquaintance from his Jacobinism, but was repelled by his eccentricity.' As to his departure from Oxford, the legend is only so far wrong, that he shot at a closed shutter of a Fellow's room, not at the Fellow—

that he was rusticated not expelled ; that his tutor,
'dear good Bennett,' cried at the sentence ; and
that the President invited him to return in the
name of all the Fellows except one, who afterwards, Landor wrote to Southey, ' proved for the
first time his honesty and justice by hanging himself.' The acceptance of this proposal was not
likely to be entertained ; and now the grave question arose, to what profession was this singular
youth to attach himself? In later years Landor
used to relate that he had been offered a commission in the Army on the preposterous terms ' that
he should keep his opinions to himself,' which he
naturally declined ; that then his father proposed
to give him four hundred a year if he would read
for the bar, but he expressed his horror of Law and
Lawyers so plainly that that transaction was soon at
an end. It does not appear, however, that any of
these alternatives were seriously offered or refused.
It was too evident that young Landor, the heir to
a considerable entailed estate, was not likely to
settle down to any fixed course of professional
life. Mr. Forster seems to regret that the boy
had not been brought up with some such definite
intention ; but it appears to me very doubtful
whether any such discipline would not have done

4

more harm than good. It is difficult to imagine him successful in any career but that which he voluntarily adopted. With his contempt for the ordinary operations of society ; with his candour in hatred of all that differed from him ; with his reversed Utopia of an extinct world, where Philosophers and Poets were, and where Kings and Parliaments were not, and with his pride that no success could satisfy, how could he have ever become the fair competitor or just antagonist of other men ? Assuredly, even for his moral being, he found the best place in the open field of Literature, where, though he was fond of saying ' that the only use of study was the prevention of idleness, otherwise the learning other people's opinions only corrupts your own,' he nevertheless developed a considerable amount of intellectual sympathy, and formed solid attachments which clung to him through the troubles and accidents of his wayward life.

The continuous and lonely study of the three years which, with an occasional visit to Warwick, he spent at Tenby and Swansea, formed his literary character. Years afterwards he used to dream with delight of the sandy shore of Southern Wales, with its dells and dingles covered with moss-roses

and golden snapdragons. The small allowance
he received from his family was fully sufficient for
the simplicity and thrift of that almost pastoral
mode of existence ; and he often expressed his
gratitude to the vigilant wreckers of the West,
who kept him supplied with excellent claret from
the unfortunate French merchantmen that ran
upon the shore. There he matured his previous
knowledge by a complete review of the relics of the
old Roman world, and added to his familiarity
with Greek, of which, however, he never attained
an entire mastery. There, too, he modified, by
application to the elder English classics, the admiration which he had hitherto, by a congeniality of
taste, exclusively lavished on the writers of the
age of Anne. ' My prejudices in favour of ancient
literature,' he writes, ' began to wear away on
" Paradise Lost," and even the great hexameter
sounded to me tinkling, when I had recited aloud,
in my solitary walks on the sea-shore, the haughty
appeal of Satan and the repentance of Eve.' Mr.
Forster has unburied ' A Moral Epistle to Earl
Stanhope,' of which I regret that he has only
given some effective fragments. These and earlier
poems of Landor have a premature completeness,
which rather assimilates them to the ' Windsor

Forest' of Pope than to the fluent puerilities of
Byron or Shelley. They are quite good as far
as they go. In his Satire he does not always
adhere to that graceful definition of his later days,
that 'the smile is habitual to her countenance;
she has little to do with Philosophy, less with
Rhetoric, and nothing with the Furies:' but his
political censorship is mild for those times of
licentious speech and despotic repression. His
allusions to the humour of Sophocles singularly
anticipate the acute Essay of the present Bishop
of St. David's on the irony of that dramatist in
the 'Museum Philologicum,' and, in his application
of the lines—

ὅδ' ἐστὶν ἡμῶν ναυκράτωρ ὁ παῖς, ὅσ' ἂν
οὗτος λέγῃ σοι, ταῦτά σοι χἠμεῖς φαμέν—

to the Boy-pilot 'who weathered the storm,' he
almost prefigures the future National Song. He
ends the dedication to the Radical peer by la-
menting 'that Fortune should have placed on his
brow the tinsel coronet instead of the civic wreath;
—for himself, she had nothing to give, because
there was nothing he would ask: he would rather
have an Executioner than a Patron.'

After the production of much social verse of

remarkable concinnity, he now for the first time set himself to write a serious and sustained poem, and in 1798 published ' Gebir,' or ' Gebirus '—we use the words indifferently, for so was the work composed, in English or in Latin as the fancy swayed him ; and I do not know which was finished first, though the Latin was given to the public later. The design of the story is hardly worth inquiring into, for story there is none ; it is a series of romantic pictures, wonderful in expression, and many of them beautiful in design. I will not repeat, out of respect for Landor's ghost, the passage of the ' echoing sea-shell,' the prominence of which in popular remembrance always seemed to him a sort of intimation of the oblivion of the rest of the poem ; but I would willingly recall to the present generation, forgetful of their great predecessors, such a sweep of Heroic Verse as the Sixth Book, the aërial ' Nuptial Voyage of the Morning,'—

> pointed out by Fate
> When an immortal maid and mortal man
> Should share each other's nature, knit in bliss.

Still there was nothing in the work that could hope to catch the popular ear. Even to the lovers of the supernatural Eld the poem had little but

poetic attractions, and these require the corre-
sponding magnet.   It had not the divine serenity
of Wordsworth's 'Laodamia,' nor the majestic
wail of Swinburne's 'Atalanta.'   In the preface,
indeed, the author earnestly deprecated any vulgar
favour.   'If there are now in England ten men of
taste and genius who will applaud my poem, I
declare myself fully content.   I will call for a
division.   I shall count a majority.'   The City was
saved—the Ten Just Men were found.   'Gebir' was
sent to Dr. Parr with a characteristic letter, suggesting that, while Parr was examining his verse,
the writer would feel much like Polydorus, whose
tomb, once turfed and spruce and flourishing, was
plucked for a sacrifice to Æneas.'   This note the
dogmatic Doctor superscribed, 'A most ingenious
man,' and wrote later on the title-page of 'Gebirus,' 'The work of a Scholar and a Poet.'   Southey
wrote to Cottle, 'There is a poem called "Gebir,"
of which I know not whether my review of it in
the "Critical" be yet printed; but in that review
you will find some of the most exquisite poetry in
the language.   I would go a hundred miles to see
the (anonymous) author.'   Again to Coleridge, on
starting for Lisbon : 'I take with me for the
voyage your poems—the "Lyrics," the "Lyrical

Ballads," and "Gebir." These make all my library.
I like "Gebir" more and more.' And once more
to Davy, 'The lucid passages of "Gebir" are
all palpable to the eye ; they are the master-touches
of a painter. There is power in them and passion
and thought and knowledge.' Coleridge seems to
have been attracted at first, but became annoyed
at what he considered his friend's over-praise.
Though with this and other such select approbation Landor professed himself fully satisfied, the
inevitable yearning of a poet, however self-con-
tented, for a larger sympathy was clearly strong
within him. Some time after he alluded to the
possibility of his having been a successful writer
in early life, and to the colour that such a contin-
gency might have given to his whole existence, and
gently confesses that there is 'a pleasure in the
hum of summer insects.'

In answer to a somewhat contemptuous article
in the 'Monthly Review,' he planned a prose postscript to 'Gebir,' which, somehow or other, was
suppressed—as strong a piece of scornful and witty
writing as he ever uttered, to judge from the extracts of it which Mr. Forster has given. In this
essay he remarks on the decline of the interest in
poetry in English society since the days when even

such poets as Parnell and Mallet were carefully
read, and when Johnson thought versifiers unworthy the corner of a provincial newspaper fit
objects for his philosophical biography. Surely
this criterion will hardly seem just to those who
recall with wonder and envy the culture and enjoyment of poetry in the upper classes manifested
in the early years of this century, when the clubs
resounded with ' Marmion,' and Rogers rose to
fashion on the ' Pleasures of Memory.' The very
acrimony with which the novel simplicity of Wordsworth and the dim idealism of Coleridge were
then received was rather the antagonism of a rival
school than a proof of any neglect of the Art.
There is the same interpretation to be given to the
succeeding reputations of Shelley and Keats as
contrasted with those of Byron, Scott, Crabbe,
and Moore. The best poetry certainly was only
welcomed by a ' little clan,' and for awhile unheard,

> Save of the quiet primrose, and the span
> Of Heaven, and few ears ; *

but that too, made its way in due time, while the
verse that appealed to a wider range of sympathy

---

* Keats.

and passions was the daily sustenance and delight
even of the higher portion of good society which
did not lay claim to any especial intellectual distinction.   In our day, by a strange diversion, these
tastes, like the concurrent interests of pictorial art,
find their recipients not in the leisurely class which
one would suppose to be especially educated in
their cultivation, but in the busy builders of the
mercantile and commercial wealth of the country
and their own.

‘ Gebir ’ was followed by other small volumes of
English and Latin verse, and separate pieces
printed in the quarto fashion of the day, of which
Mr. Rogers always spoke as a great defence
against loose and unstudied verse. ‘ Any man
becomes critical of his own writings when they
stand in large type before him.’ But we soon
meet Landor in a very novel and uncongenial
character—as a contributor to the public press.
The main instigator to this employment of his
talents was, no doubt, his friend Parr, and the in-
termediary agent a stirring politician of the time,
whom this generation yet remembers as a pleasant
Whig veteran—Sir Robert Adair. Landor and
Adair meeting at Debrett's in Piccadilly, and going
down to the House of Commons—‘ the most costly

4*

exhibition in Europe,' as the young poet stigma-
tised it—and the former having access to the re-
porters' gallery to prepare himself for the 'Courier,'
are as anomalous positions as can well be imagined.
The tone in which he meets his new clients is about
as conciliatory as that in which he confronted his
literary compeers.

'I never court the vulgar,' he writes to Parr:
'and how immense a majority of every rank and
description this happy word comprises! Perhaps
about thirty in the universe may be expected, and
never more at a time. But I know how to value
the commendation you bestow on me; for though
I have not deserved it, nor so largely, yet it will
make me attempt to conquer my idleness, my disgust, and to reach it some time or other. You
will find that I have taken courage to follow the
path you pointed out, in pursuing the Execrable.
(Pitt.) I subjoin my letter. At present I have
not sent it to the printer, though it has been
finished a fortnight. The reason is this: I wrote
one a thousand times better than the present,
in which I aimed my whole force at a worse man
than P.—there are only two—and it was not W.
(Wyndham), and I sent it for insertion to the
" Courier." Now, such is my indifference, that

when once I have written anything, I never in-
quire for it afterwards; and this was the case in
respect to my letter. I have not seen the
" Courier " since, but I have some suspicion that it
was not inserted.'

Nor was he in better accord with the traditions
and the men of his party. ' Some of the Whigs,'
he used to say, ' are made honest men by their
interests. Tories are proud, Whigs insolent.' By
an especial crotchet he had in ' Gebir ' made a
monster of the Whig Hero of 1688—

> What tyrant with more insolence e'er claimed
> Dominion? when from th' heart of Usury
> Rose more intense the pale-flamed thirst for gold?
> And called forsooth *Deliverer !* False or fools
> Who praised the dull-eared miscreant, or who hoped
> To soothe your folly and disgrace with praise—

and the great Liberal leader of his own time fell
so short of his ideal that he could not heartily
make a hero of him, and nothing less satisfied him
or checked the asperities of his criticism. To his
rival, indeed, he bore an absolute abhorrence,
which he retained to his last days, without any limit
or concession. When questioned as to Mr. Pitt's
oratory, he would say, ' It was a wonderful thing
to hear, but I have seen others more wonderful—

a fire-eater, and a man who eat live rats.' Of his neglect of wealth, ' Few people have sixty millions a year to spend : he spent on himself just what he chose, and gave away what he chose.' Pitt's negotiations with the Irish for Emancipation he assumed to be a diabolical treachery,—the minister being assured of the Sovereign's determination not to cede the point in question. The French war he described as ' a plot to make England a waste, to drive the gentry by war-taxes to taverns, and hells, and clubs, and transfer their wealth and position to the mercantile interest.' After Mr. Fox's death, indeed, he was inclined to a milder judgment of the Whig chief, and a ' Commentary ' on Trotter's ' Memoirs' (printed 1812) contains perhaps more fair and moderate political and literary judgments, delivered in his own humour, than any work of his earlier or maturer years. There seems no sufficient reason, even in those susceptible days, why this essay should have been suppressed ; but it was in fact so entirely wasted, (in the old printers' phrase) that I believe I possess the only existing copy, which he sent to Southey. It should be reprinted in any new edition of his collected works. It contains many vigorous passages applicable to the contests and difficulties of our own day, though the style is far from the perfection he attained in his later writings. In vindicating a juster government of Ireland, irrespective of its religion, he inquires indignantly, and with an amusing reference to India, 'Of what consequence is it to us if the Irish choose to worship a cow or a potato?' And adverting to the question of Emancipation, 'If all the members returned were Catholics, still what harm could they do?' In the dedication to Washington there is a passage that might be addressed to President Grant :

'Your importance, your influence, and, I believe, your wishes, rest entirely on the comforts and happiness of your people. A declaration of hostilities against Great Britain would much and grievously diminish them, however popular it might be in the commencement, however glorious it might be in the result. My apprehension lest this popularity should in any degree sway your mind is the sole cause by which I am determined in submitting to you these considerations. Popularity in a free state like yours, where places are not exposed to traffic, nor dignities to accident, is a legitimate and noble desire ; and the prospects of territory are to nations growing rich and powerful what the hopes of progeny are to individuals of rank and station.   A war between America and England would at all times be a civil war.   Our origin, our language, our interests are the same. Would it not be deplorable—would it not be intolerable to reason and humanity—that the language of a Locke and a Milton should convey and retort the sentiments of a Bonaparte and a Robespierre ? '

So say we to-day; though the thought has sometimes come across public men whether our relations with the United States would not be more stable and more happy if we did not speak the same language, if we did not understand and attend to everything disagreeable and untoward that is said or written on either side, if we had not all the accompaniments and conditions of family ties, in the sense in which Mr. Rogers answered some one who spoke of a distinguished literary fraternity as being ' like brothers,'—' I had heard they were not well together, but did not know it was so bad as that.'

With all his harsh and rash condemnations Landor had a constant tenderness for amiable people.   He often repeated, ' No man is thoroughly bad unless he is unkind.'   Thus side by side with such assaults on Mr. Fox as—

' To the principles of a Frenchman he added the habits of a Malay, in idleness, drunkenness, and gaming ; in middle life he was precisely the opposite of whoever was in power, until he could spring forward to the same station. Whenever Mr. Pitt was wrong, Mr. Fox was right, and then only '— stand such sentences as—

' Mr. Fox in private life was a most sincere and amiable man ; if he suppressed in society a part of his indignant feelings, as a man so well bred would do, he never affected a tone of cordiality towards those whom he reprobated or despised.'

Again, in a letter to the ' Examiner,' in 1850, he writes of him, ' He had more and warmer friends than any statesman on record ; he was ingenuous, liberal, learned, philosophical ; he was the delight of social life, the ornament of domestic.'

In the ' Epitaphium C. Foxii ' this double feeling has a charming expression :—

> Torrens eloquio inque præpotentes
> Iracundus et acer, et feroci
> Vultu vinculaque et cruces minatus,
> Placandus tamen ut catellus æger
> Qui morsu digitum petit protervum ꓉
> Et lambit decies : tuis amicis
> Tantum carior in dies et horas
> Quantum deciperes magis magisque :
> O Foxi lepide, o miselle Foxi,

Ut totus penitusque deperisti !
Tu nec fallere nec potes jocari,
Tu nec ludere, mane vesperive;
Quà nemo cubitum quatit, quiescis,
Jacta est alea : conticet fritillus.

I will conclude my extracts from the 'Commentary'
with a passage in which the transition from irony
to solemnity seems to me remarkably effective :—

'I have nothing to say on any man's religion;
and, indeed, where a man is malignant in his words
or actions his creed is unimportant to others and
unavailing to himself. But I grieve whenever a kind
heart loses any portion of its comforts; and Dr. Parr,
I am certain, felt the deepest sorrow that Mr. Fox
wanted any that Christianity could give. Whether
in the Established Church the last consolations of
religion are quite so impressive and efficacious;
whether they always are administered with the
same earnestness and tenderness as the parent
Church administers them, is a question which
I should deem it irreverent to discuss. Certainly he is happiest in his death, whose fortitude
is most confiding and most peaceful: whose
composure rests not merely on the suppression
of doubts and fears: whose pillow is raised
up, whose bosom is lightened, whose mortality
is loosened from him, by an assemblage of all

consolatory hopes, indescribable, indistinguish-
able, indefinite, yet surer than ever were the
senses.'

It is agreeable to turn to the rare gleams of
satisfaction and approbation in Landor's political
controversy. Of Lord Rockingham he was wont
to speak with invariable respect; but it is for the
memory of Sir Samuel Romilly that he preserved
the most reverent affection; he made him the in-
terlocutor in two admirable dialogues, and wrote of
him, in one mention out of many :—

'He went into public life with temperate and
healthy aspirations; Providence having blessed
him with domestic peace, withheld him from
political animosities. He knew that the soundest
fruits grew near the ground, and he waited for the
higher to fall into his bosom, without an effort or a
wish to seize on them. No man whosoever in our
parliamentary history has united, in more perfect
accordance and constancy, pure virtue and lofty
wisdom.'

He loved to compare Romilly and Phocion, and
composed a pathetic inscription, which might well
be placed upon his tomb.

One injustice, now remedied in the person of his
distinguished son, is pleasantly recorded :—

' No one ever thought of raising Romilly to the peerage, although never was a gentleman of his profession respected more highly or more universally. . . . The reason could not be that already too many of it had entered the House of Lords; since every wind of every day had blown bellying silk-gowns to that quarter, and under the highest walls of Westminster was moored a long galley of lawyers, chained by the leg to their Administrations; some designated by the names of - fishing-towns and bathing machines they had never entered, and others of hamlets and farms they had recently invaded.'

In these notices I have somewhat anticipated the course of Landor's life. On the death of his father in 1805 he came into a good property, and took up his residence at Bath, where he lived somewhat ostentatiously and beyond his means, moving a good deal in society, but singularly annoyed by the inferiority of his dancing. He told his son ' he had lost more pleasure by being a bad dancer than anything else; ' and it is intelligible that any grace which he could not realise must have been a trouble to him. But this conventional existence was interrupted by a resolve to join the British army in Spain in 1808. Not only had he partaken of the

passionate delight of Wordsworth and Coleridge
and Southey in those days when—

> Bliss was it in the dawn to be alive,
> But to be young was very Heaven,

but his hopes had then a centre in the young Hero
in whom he thought he saw the embodied Revolution. In 'Gebir' he had represented him as θεότοκος,

> A mortal man above all mortal praise;

and afterwards, when, instead of the liberator of the
world, the restorer of order developed himself in all
the unscrupulous ambition of which the history of
M. Lanfrey is at this moment giving the most recent and faithful portraiture, the revulsion of feeling
in Landor's mind was as absolute as might be expected. He soon came to believe that Bonaparte
'had the fewest virtues and the faintest semblances
of them of any man that had risen by his own
efforts to supreme power;' and, though he continually rejoiced in his work of destruction of the old
governments, yet he never lost sight of the moral
obliquity of the agent. That supernatural intellectual activity, that multitudinousness of ideas, which
the publication of his 'Correspondence' has revealed,
was then so little appreciated even by his adulators,

that it is no discredit to Landor to have under-
rated his faculties; and he was too happy to find
in its supreme head a vindication of his indomitable
hatred of the French nation, which had 'spoiled
everything it had touched, even Liberty,'—'where
everything was ugly, Men, Women, Dogs, even the
Sky,'—'a set of mischievous children whom you
may beat as you will one day, and they will forget
and deny it the next.' There was no personal
atrocity, indeed, of which he did not think Napoleon capable; he had no doubt of the murder
of Captain Wright in the prisons of Paris, nor
of that of Colonel Bathurst in the fortress of
Magdeburg.* But his anxiety to see the Man,
and still more the 'spolia opima' of art in Paris,
took him to Paris in 1802. Mr. Forster's accounts
of the occasions on which he saw the First Consul
are hard to reconcile with an incident he was
fond of relating that 'he met Bonaparte walking
in the Tuileries garden, and the fellow looked at
him so insolently that, if he had not had a lady on
his arm, he would have knocked him down.' This

---

* Colonel Bathurst, son of the Bishop of Norwich, British envoy
to Vienna, disappeared unaccountably in the forest of Boitzenburg
in the neighbourhood of Hamburg, during the war, and was never
heard of again.

may well have been a romance of memory, for he persuaded himself that he had seen the fugitive Emperor at Tours in 1815 in the person of a wearied horseman dismounting in the courtyard of the Préfet's house, the door of which was suddenly closed on him the day he was supposed to have traversed that city. Thus, when the invasion of Spain had provoked the English intervention which resulted in the fall of the conqueror, less enthusiastic natures than Landor's were excited to share its perils and its glories. When Mr. Graham (the future Lord Lynedoch) led forth his clansmen from Scotland and Sir Watkin Wynn his tenants from Wales, there was nothing surprising in a poet and political writer with an independent fortune joining the British forces as a volunteer. At first all went well; he presented 10,000 reals to the burnt and pillaged town of Venturada, and set about enrolling a troop of a thousand Spaniards to join the army of General Blake. For this he received from the Central Junta the honorary rank of Colonel; but Landor's temperament was not likely to be proof against the contingencies of any disciplined service. The English Envoy, Sir Charles Stuart, said something affronting about somebody, which Landor interpreted against him-

self, and wrote a furious letter, and printed it in
both languages, before any reply was possible.
Then came the Convention of Cintra, one of those
political compromises which imaginative men were
sure to abhor ; and he retired in a passion of disgust. 'Can we never be disgraced,' he writes to
Southey, 'but the only good people in the world
must witness it ?' and the gentle Southey answers,
'Break the terms, and deliver up the wretch who
signed it (Sir Hew Dalrymple) to the French with
a rope round his neck : this is what Oliver Cromwell would have done.' The only useful outcome
of this adventure to Landor was his 'Tragedy of
Count Julian,' a more complete work than any he
had yet produced, and of which there has been no
truer criticism than that of De Quincey, who, after
describing Landor as dilating like Satan into
Teneriffe or Atlas, when he sees before him an
antagonist worthy of his prowess, concludes : 'That
sublimity of penitential grief, which cannot accept
consolation from man, cannot bear external reproach, cannot condescend to notice insult, cannot so
much as see the curiosity of bystanders ; that awful
carelessness of all but the troubled deep within his
own heart, and of God's spirit brooding upon their
surface and searching their abysses—never was so

majestically described.'   Two lines of the closing
scene dwell on the memory :—

> 'Of all who pass us in Life's drear descent
>   We grieve the most for those who wished to die.'

This Tragedy the house of Longman declined even
to print at the author's expense !   Little did they
imagine the effect of this refusal.   Landor threw
another poem into the fire and renounced the
literary career for ever.   He writes to Southey,
' You cannot imagine how I feel relieved at laying
down its burden and abandoning this tissue of
humiliations.'   An unexpected deliverer appeared
in the hostile camp of the ' Quarterly Review,' and
Mr. Murray accepted the poem, which, however, no
more touched the popular taste than its predecessors.

The project of marriage was not unfamiliar to
Landor's mind.   In 1808 he wrote to Southey :—

' I should have been a good and happy man if I
had married.   My heart is tender.   I am fond of
children and of talking childishly.   I hate even to
travel two stages.   Never without a pang do I leave
the house where I was born.   .   .   .   I do not say
I shall never be happy ; I shall be often so if I live ;
but I shall never be at rest.   My evil genius dogs

me through existence, against the current of my best inclinations. I have practised self-denial, because it gives me a momentary and false idea that I am firm ; and I have done other things not amiss in compliance with my heart : but my most virtuous hopes and sentiments have uniformly led to misery, and I have never been happy, but in consequence of some weakness or vice.'

His feeling for female beauty was intense. 'Women,' he would say, 'pay dearly for expression : English women have no expression ; they are therefore so beautiful.' Thus no wonder that in 1811 he announces to his friend that the evening of beginning to transcribe his tragedy he 'fell in love with a girl without a sixpence, and with few accomplishments ; she is pretty, graceful, and good-tempered, three things indispensable to my happiness ;' and he assures his mother, 'she has no pretensions of any kind, and her want of fortune was the very thing which determined me to marry her.' The lady's name was Thuillier,* of an ancient Swiss family. He sent Parr some Alcaics on the occasion, and the veteran returned an ardent

* The family are now represented by the distinguished artillery officer Col. R. E. Landor Thuillier, F.R.S., Surveyor-General of India.

congratulation, and a Latin poem against the Government.

By this time Landor had become a resident Squire. He had sold the old family properties, and bought, at the time when land was dearest, a ruined abbey in the northern angle of Monmouthshire, at the cost of some 60,000*l.* Colonel Wood had fitted up the southern tower as a shooting-box, and this was the only residence when Landor established himself there in 1809. In his own words, ' Llanthony was a noble estate, eight miles long, and produced everything but herbage, corn, and money.' He planted a million trees (among them a wood of cedars of Lebanon), of which a small tithe are still visible. The valley in which the abbey stood had been celebrated in Drayton's ' Polyolbion' as one

> ' Which in it such a shape of solitude doth bear
> As Nature at the first appointed it for prayer ; '

– not a promising situation to build a country-house in and bring a young wife to. Under the most fortunate circumstances it is difficult to imagine Landor a comfortable Country Gentleman. For field sports, in which the unoccupied upper classes of this country expend harmlessly so much of the

superfluous energy and occasional savagery of their
dispositions, he had no taste.   In his youth he had
shot a partridge one winter afternoon, and found
the bird alive the next morning, after a night of
exceptional bitterness.   'What that bird must
have suffered!' he exclaimed.   'I often think of its
look,' and never took gun in hand again.   For the
pastoral pleasure of farming he was much too im-
petuous, and had to depend entirely on others for
the management of the estate.   In this he was
characteristically unlucky.   He went to Southey
for advice as to a tenant, and took one whom the
more practical brother poet knew to be totally unfit
—a petty officer of the East Indian service, without capital and entirely ignorant of agriculture.
The family are immortalised in a letter of Charles
Lamb's :—'I know all your Welsh annoyances—
the measureless B——s.   I know a quarter of a
mile of them—seventeen brothers and sixteen
sisters, as they appear to me in memory.   There
was one of them that used to fix his long legs on
my fender and tell a story of a shark every night,
endless, immortal.   How have I grudged the salt-
sea ravener not having had his gorge of him!'   It
was this family of land-sharks who set upon Landor
and turned him out of house and home.   As a

landlord he seems to have been generous, even lavish, and when driven to law for the payment of rent was foiled by the low ingenuities of country practice, till he wrote—

Hinc nempe tantum ponderis leges habent
Quam natione barbara degentibus.
Est noxa nulla præter innocentiam ;
Tutisque vivitur omnibus præter probos.

The damage to his trees through carelessness or malice affected him deeply. 'We recover from illness,' he writes, ' we build palaces, we retain or change the features of the earth at pleasure, excepting that only the whole of human life cannot replace one bough.' In the midst of this turmoil, when he looked on himself as food for the spoiler, the Duke of Beaufort declined to make him a magistrate. This was hardly surprising after his behaviour on the Grand Jury at the previous sessions, when he personally presented to the Judge a bill that his colleagues had ignored ; but when he politely desired the appointment of some person of more information than himself for the protection of the neighbourhood, his application should hardly have remained unanswered. He then had recourse to the Lord Chancellor, with the same issue. I do not understand whether a second letter, which

Mr. Forster gives, was actually sent, but it is so clever and so inappropriate a composition, that it may have been taken as a complete vindication of the Duke's refusal. Then, or later, Landor hung up for posterity his effigy of Lord Eldon :

Officiosus . erga . omnes . potentes . præter . Deum .
Quem . satis . ei . erat . adjurare.

I have never heard any authentic account of the immediate cause of Landor's abandonment of his country. Mention has been made of his knocking down in court a barrister who seemed to doubt his word ; and some question of outlawry occurs with regard to a frivolous suit, of which, however, no further notice seems to have been taken. Landor certainly thought his own and his wife's persons in danger at Llanthony, and his embarrassments were such as to make a temporary removal expedient ; but the Court of Exchequer decided finally in his favour against his defaulting tenants, and the estate in competent hands would soon have given, and indeed did give him, a fair income. He certainly detested our climate. ' You may live in England,' he said, ' if you are rich enough to have a solar system of your own, not without.' However, in May 1814, he passed over to Jersey, where Mrs.

Landor joined him with one of her sisters. There occurred the first open breach in his matrimonial relations. After some imprudent words on her side, he rose early, walked across the island, and embarked alone in an oyster-boat for France. Hence he wrote to Southey that he reserved to himself 160*l.* per annum, and left his wife the rest of his fortune. He tells him of 'the content and moderation which she had always preserved in the midst of penury and seclusion,' but adds that 'every kind and tender sentiment is rooted up from his heart for ever.' There is a terrible consciousness of his own infirmity in the conclusion : 'She gave me my first headache, which every irritation renews. It is an affection of the brain only, and it announces to me that my end will be the most miserable and humiliating.' I will place this sentence by the side of one of the very latest of his poems, with a sense of its impressive reality. In November 1863, when his last volume ('Heroic Idylls') was in the press, he sent the following pathetic lines to be inserted, but the volume was already made-up : and they did not appear in print.

TO ONE ILL-MATED.

We all wish many things undone
Which now the heart lies heavy on.
You should indeed have longer tarried
On the roadside before you married,
And other flowers have picked or past,
Before you singled out your last.
Many have left the search with sighs
Who sought for hearts and found but eyes.
The brightest stars are not the best
To follow in the way to rest.

It is small reproach to any woman that she did not possess a sufficient union of charm, tact, and intelligence to suit Landor as a wife. He demanded beauty in woman as imperatively as honesty in men, yet was hardly submissive to its influence ; just as, while he was intolerant to folly, he would have been impatient of any competing ability. Therefore, eloquent as is his pleading in the following passage, and just as is the general observation, it must be taken only as the partial aspect of his own domestic calamity :

'It often happens that if a man unhappy in the married state were to describe the manifold causes of his uneasiness, it would be found by those who were beyond their influence to be of such a nature as rather to excite derision than sympathy. The

waters of bitterness do not fall on his head in a
cataract, but through a colander—one, however,
like the vases of the Danaïdes, perforated only for
replenishment.   We know scarcely the vestibule of
a house of which we fancy we have perforated all
the corners.   We know not how grievously a man
may have suffered, long before the calumnies of
the world befell him, as he reluctantly left his
house-door.   There are women from whom incessant tears of anger swell forth at imaginary wrongs;
but of contrition for their own delinquencies not
one.'

A reconciliation followed on the present occasion which seems to have been as complete as circumstances and temper made possible.   After they
had settled at Como, the birth of his first child
gave him infinite pleasure.   He called him Arnold
Savage, after the second Speaker of the House of
Commons, whom he somewhere read to have
declared ' that grievances should be redressed before
money should be granted,' and with whom he
claimed what was probably a problematical relation-
ship.   I have been told that when the question
of the decoration of the Houses of Parliament
was first started, he informed Lord John Russell of
his expectation that his illustrious ancestor should

receive due recognition, and that he received an
answer to the effect that Lord John had not yet
obtained any assurance that the patriotic devotion
of his own relative William Lord Russell would be
recorded on the walls of the Palace of Westminster.

The Princess of Wales resided at this time at the
Villa d'Este, where her conduct was so flagrant that
Landor was surprised that her husband did not
sue for a divorce. When, at a later period, his
name was brought forward in connection with the
evidence he could give on the trial, he wrote to the
' Times : ' ' The secrets of the bedchamber and of
the escritoire have never been the subjects of my
investigation. During my residence on the Lake
of Como my time was totally occupied in literary
pursuits ; and I believe no man of that character
was ever thought worthy of employment by the
present Administration. Added to which I was
insulted by an Italian domestic of the Queen, and
I demanded from her in vain the punishment of
the aggressor ; this alone, which might create and
keep alive the most active resentment in many
others, would impose eternal silence on me.' He
one day confirmed this in conversation, concluding
in his grand manner, ' If I had known anything
good of her after her behaviour to me, I should of

course have been bound to go to England at my own expense and state it on her trial.'

I have already alluded to his subsequent ejection from Lombardy ; no unlikely event when we remember what was then the Austrian rule, and that he always designated the Emperor as ' the man who had betrayed his own patriot Hofer into the hands of the French, and sold his own daughter to a Corsican robber.' He would say, ' Men who, like Francis, have no sympathies with their kin, should be put to live with hyenas.'

At Pisa a girl was born to him, and he wrote a touching letter to his mother asking her to be sponsor :—

' The misery of not being able to see you is by far the greatest I have ever suffered. Never shall I forget the thousand acts of kindness and affection I have received from you from my earliest to my latest days. . . . As, perhaps, I may never have another, I shall call my little Julia by the name of Julia Elizabeth Savage Landor, and, with your permission, will engage some one of Julia's English friends to represent you. This is the first time I was ever a whole day without seeing Arnold. I wonder what his thought are on the occasion. Mine are a great deal more about him than about

5*

the house I most look for. He is of all living
creatures the most engaging, and already repeats
ten of the most beautiful pieces of Italian poetry.
The honest priest, his master, says he is a miracle
and a marvel, and exceeds in abilities all he ever
saw or heard of. What a pity it is that such divine
creatures should ever be men, and subject to regrets and sorrows!'

This is written from Florence, where he soon
fixed himself on the Palazzo Medici, and where the
great literary enterprise which had for some time
possessed his thoughts was undertaken and accomplished. The one continuous link with his native
country, that had remained unbroken through
these wandering years, had been his correspondence with Southey. That friendship between
natures apparently so incompatible had been
hardly affected, and certainly not lessened in the
main, by the extremest divergence of opinion.
This relation between the writer of the ' Vision of
Judgment' and the open advocate of regicide, between the author of the ' Book of the Church' and
the adorer of the old Gods, between the diffuse romantic poet and the close Roman epigrammatist,
between the decorous moralist and the apologist of
the Cæsars, is a signal and instructive example of

the happy intimacy and mutual comfort that may exist between men of genius, who are drawn together by heartfelt admiration and enjoyment of each other's powers, and a determination to find out, and hold by, all possible points of sympathy and common interest, letting the rest drop out of sight and all that is not congenial be forgotten. The tender intimacy that existed in later days between Landor and the reverent, fervent, spirit of Julius Hare, was a further illustration of the capacities of intellectual sympathy; and I should be content to refer those who have been wont to look on Landor as an ill-conditioned misanthrope to Southey, after almost every name had passed from his perception, repeating softly to himself, 'Landor, my Landor;' and to Archdeacon Hare, two days before his death, murmuring, 'Dear Landor, I hope we shall meet once more.' It had been Southey's habit for many years to add to the literary toils of his ill-requited profession the careful transcription in his dainty hand-writing of his poems as he composed them, canto after canto, for Landor's perusal and criticism. He also kept him duly informed of the course of his prose writings, and had told him of his proposed dialogues on 'The Condition of Society,' the plan of which had originally grown out of 'Boethius.' These 'Conversations' were entirely consecutive, and the only interlocutors were himself and Sir Thomas More, 'who recognises in me,' Southey writes, 'some dis-pathies, but more points of agreement.' The notion had clearly touched Landor's imagination, and it is evident how much there was in this form of composition which was cognate to both his intellectual and moral peculiarities. His dominant self-assertion seized with delight a form in which it could constantly reproduce itself in the most diverse shapes, in which every paradox could be freely stated and every platitude boldly contradicted—in which, under the names he most loved and most abhorred, he could express his admiration and his hatred—in which exaggeration was legitimate, and accuracy superfluous. The literary character of the plan has never been better drawn than in Mr. Forster's language :—

' All the leading shapes of the past, the most familiar and the most august, were to be called up again. Modes of thinking the most various, and events the most distant, were proposed for his theme. Beside the fires of the present, the ashes of the past were to be rekindled and to shoot again into warmth and brightness. The scene was to be shifting as life, but continuous as time. Down it were to pass successions of statesmen, lawyers, and churchmen; wits and men of letters; party men, soldiers, and kings; the most tender, delicate, and noble women; figures fresh from the schools of Athens and the courts of Rome; philosophers philosophizing, and politicians discussing questions of state; poets talking of poetry, men of the world of matters worldly, and English, Italians, and French of their respective literatures and manners. . . . The requisites for it were such as no other existing writer possessed in the same degree as he did. Nothing had been indifferent to him that affected humanity. Poetry and history had delivered up to him their treasures, and the secrets of antiquity were his.'

About the time when the first Income Tax was imposed, Landor had written one 'Conversation' between Lord Grenville and Burke, and another between Henry IV. and Sir Arnold Savage; the first he had offered to the 'Morning Chronicle,' but it was refused as too personal. Now, in March 1822 he had written fifteen new ones, having rejected one between Swift and Sir William Temple as too democratical (what must it have been?), and another between Addison and Lord Somers as too

maliciously critical of the supposed purist's in-
elegancies and inaccuracies of style, 'the number
of which surpasses belief.' These, when aug-
mented to twenty-three, formed the MS. trans-
mitted through Captain Vyner to the House of
Messrs. Longman, which entirely declined their
publication; but the kind activity of Mr. Julius
Hare, with whom Landor had become acquainted
through his brother Francis, actually forced Mr.
Taylor, the publisher of the 'London Magazine,'
to undertake the work.

The brothers Hare were all men of mark.
The elder, Francis, well known as a man about
town by the sobriquet of the 'Hare of many
Friends,' had been brought up in Italy under
the care of Professor (afterwards Cardinal) Mezzo-
fanti, and had acquired in some degree the linguistic powers of his preceptor. He could talk to
every Italian in his own dialect, and knew the appropriate saints to adjure in every Italian village.
In his own language, though he wrote little, if anything, besides some contributions to the 'Edinburgh
Review,' he displayed a facility of expression as
various and as monopolising as that of Coleridge
or Macaulay. Landor, with a tender humour, in-

corporates this peculiarity into the eulogy of his
friend :—

> Who held mute the joyous and the wise
> With wit and eloquence—whose tomb, afar
> From all his friends and all his countrymen,
> Saddens the bright Palermo.

The younger brothers, Julius and Augustus, though
each in their different styles important contributors
to English divinity, and now familiar to the
English public in their relative's admirable 'Memorials of a Quiet Life,' live mainly in the little
volumes which all the present abundance of fragmentary literature and aphoristic reflection will not
overlay, the 'Guesses at Truth.' They remain a
most interesting production of the Coleridgian era
of English thought as exhibited in two very original
minds, so full of sound knowledge and deep wit, that
we can forgive such oddities as the junction of the
names of Landor, Bacon, and Jacob Boehme being
presented as proper objects of our admiration.

Julius became indeed to Landor's mature life all
that Southey had been to his youth, and never
permitted any the wildest overflow of opinion or
extravagance of conduct to diminish his reverence
and affection. On this occasion he performed his
editorial functions so scrupulously, that when the

prohibition or the retention of one word was said
by the publisher to make a difference of two hundred and fifty copies in the sale, he replied he had
no alternative but to leave it there; in the collected edition of 1846 Landor expunged it himself.
But the very antagonism of Hare's nature to the
lawlessness of Landor's mind enabled him to render
him a service of peculiar value in the reception of
the book. He knew well the temper of the time,
which, by assuming that all genius was the natural
enemy of public order, did a great deal to make it
so ; and which, having pilloried indiscriminately the
decorous Wordsworth and the licentious Byron,—
Hazlitt, living too much in the senses, and Shelley
too much out of them,—the grand simplicities of
Keats, and the sweet concinnities of Leigh Hunt,—
and not only these men themselves, but all their
friends, collaterals, and favourers,—had already
fixed its attention on Landor as a revolutionary
poet, and was well prepared with its materials, not
of defence, but of demolition. He therefore wrote
a double-faced review in the ' London Magazine '
of 1829, which ought to form part of the appendix
of any collected edition of Landor's works. It is
a dialogue on the Dialogues, in which the adverse
case is put with so much force and ingenuity, as

an imitation of the Landorian manner, that it quite took the sting out of the subsequent article in the Tory ' Quarterly.' On the other hand, the characteristic merits and charms of the work are portrayed in such passages as the following, where Hare describes his own feelings on the first perusal :—

' It was as if the influence of a mightier spring had been breathing through the intellectual world, loosening the chains, and thawing the ice-bound obstruction of death ; as if it had been granted to the prayers of Genius that all her favourite children should be permitted for a while to revisit the earth. They came wielding all the faculties of their minds, with the mastery they had acquired by the discipline and experience, by the exercise and combats of their lives, and arraying their thoughts in a rich, and elastic, and graceful eloquence, from which the dewy light of the opening blossom had not yet passed away. I resigned myself altogether to the impressions which thronged in upon me from everything that I heard ; for not a word was idle, not a syllable but had its due place and meaning ; if at any moment the pleasure was not unmingled, at least it was very greatly predominant throughout. If there was a good deal questionable and some things offensive in the

matter, the manner was always admirable; and
whenever a stone, against which I might have
stumbled, lay in my path, I stepped over it, or
aside from it, and would not allow myself to feel
disgust or to be irritated and stung into resistance.'

How much additional pleasure would be derived
from good literature if it was approached in this
wise and generous spirit! Hazlitt's article in the
'Edinburgh Review' shows that he had not attained it: it is appreciative of much of the literary
merit of the work, but critical of defects too evident and contradictions too flagrant to be worth
serious notice or objection. In truth, the 'Conversations' are Landor's own—dialogues with his
own mind. From the moment he formed the
design, he precluded himself from any visionary
reproduction of the personages he introduced. He
carefully restricted himself from letting any of his
actors say anything they were recorded to have
said, or placing them in any of the attitudes that
would have suggested themselves to the historical
painter. And herein lie the wonderful skill and
grace of the composition. The reader is quite
conscious that the writer has chosen the dramatic
individuality to exhibit his own opinions, instead

of the ordinary process of trying to divine what the character might or would have said; yet the sense of incongruity is rare and the impression of artificial contrivance exceptional. All fictitious dialogue is open to the objection that the book is made an instrument on which the author plays for his own diversion,—complicating, unravelling the chords as he pleases, and hardly allowing to the reader the echoes of his own judgment or discretion. He would probably like to answer the arguments adduced, or point out defects and assumptions in a very different way from the imaginary speaker, for the most honest controversialist will not always exhibit the joints of his own armour. 'I never argue with anyone except on paper,' he said, 'where there is no one to answer me.' Yet even there his 'Conversations' are not usually argumentative: the interlocutors rather sympathise than dispute, and seem to strive more to enlarge and illustrate one another's meaning than to elicit a conclusion by controversy. Landor hardly condescends to reason with himself any more than with others.

The moral relation of an author to his writings is a frequent subject of literary dispute: is there the same man at the core if we could only find him?

Which is the better or the worse, the lesser or the
greater ?   I incline to believe that a man's writings,
if of any worth ·at all, are his works indeed, and
that the best destiny he can have is to be judged
by them.   Rousseau was teaching the mothers of
France to nurse their own infants, while he was
sending his own, or at least his reputed, children
to the Foundling Hospital.   While Landor's wilful temper was making himself and all about him
unhappy, the innermost man, as reflected in his
books, was yearning for a condition of things where
all was courtesy and peace.   No one could see·him
in high and refined society without being impressed
by a dignified grace, which is just what a student
of his writings would have expected from his style.
In his Dialogues the interlocutors, however violent
in their language and savage in their judgments,
preserve towards each other a noble and respectful
demeanour such as Landor would himself have
done, or strove to do, if confronted with the objects
of his fiercest denunciation.   Though he would
assert ' that to stand at the end of a crowded street
made him burn with indignation at being a man,'—
' that he could only enjoy a theatrical representation
if he were himself the audience,'—' that when he left
the gates of his London home, he felt as a badger

would do if turned out in Cheapside,'—it was surely the truer man who wrote as follows :—

'I have never avoided the intercourse of those distinguished by virtue or genius—of genius because it warmed me and invigorated me by my trying to keep pace with it ; of virtue, that if I had any of my own, it might be called forth by such vicinity. Among all men elevated in station who have made a noise in the world (admirable expression !) I never saw in any whose presence I felt inferiority excepting Kosciusko. But how many in the lower paths of life have exerted both virtues and abilities which I never exerted and never possessed ! What strength, and courage, and perseverance in some ; in others, what endurance and moderation ! At this very moment when most, beside yourself, catching up half my words, would call and employ against me, in its ordinary signification, what ought to convey the most honorific, the term *self-sufficiency*, I bow my head before the humble, with greatly more than their humiliation.

The extravagance of Landor's political actions, whenever he came into contact with the governing portion of the world, gave the impression of a revolutionary recklessness hardly compatible with general sanity in so cultivated a mind. The open advocacy of tyrannicide as a civic duty, the indiscriminating censure of public personages, the rage against men who had raised themselves to power as well as against those born to it, the apparent hatred of law as a restraint on will, would, without his writings, have confounded him with some of the weakest and wickedest of mankind. For although they abound with passages of fierce judgments and strong denunciations, it becomes clear that, so far from abhorring power or even absolutism for its own sake, the true motives of his indignation are the malice and ignorance which render hurtful or useless to humanity those influences that ought to tend to its happiness or its development. 'What King or Prince,' he said, 'can we now address as Pliny in his Dedication did Vespasian— *Jucundissime Vespasiane?*' Before true Kingship he 'felt his mind, his very limbs, unsteady with "admiration" and somewhere' bursts forth in these fine lines—

> When shall such kings adorn the throne again?
> When the same love of what Heaven made most lovely
> Enters their hearts; when genius shines above them,
> And not beneath their feet.

It was the Courts and Cabinets, and the ordinary

incidents of Monarchy that provoked him into
such words as these:—'Kings still more bar-
barously educated than other barbarians, seeking their mirth alternately from vice and folly—
guided in their first steps of duplicity and flattery—
whatever they do but decently is worthy of applause,
whatever they do virtuously, of admiration.' His
special hatred of Bonaparte came from the thought
that he might have given the French Revolution
its true crown and consummation, have accomplished and projected its ideas, instead of merging it
in the vanities and vulgarities of common despotism.
Thus the invasion of Spain and the occupation of
the Tyrol were to him especially horrible. There
is in the Conversations a trumpet-call of Liberty
over the grave of the peasant-hero which sums up
his sense of what Napoleon was and did:—

'He was urged by no necessity, he was prompted
by no policy; his impatience of courage in an
enemy, his hatred of patriotism and integrity, in
all of which he had no idea himself and saw no
image in those about him, outstripped his blind
passion for fame, and left him nothing but power
and celebrity.'

And so too with his estimate of Aristocracy. It

was the deficiency and decline of the system, not the system itself, that annoyed him.

'When Englishmen were gentlemen the whole world seemed strewn with flowers.'

'There is no such thing now as a young gentleman.'

'When men left off wearing ruffles it looked as if their hands were cut off.'

'The English gentlemen have only the French form, like English cookery.'

'One polished man is worth a dozen wise ones; you see so much more of him.'

These and such as these were his constant expressions, and his own bearing in society carried them out. 'I should not bear to live if I forgot a man's name in his presence.' With much irony he said, 'It is now a degradation to high rank to know anything, and to impart what you know is terrible.' How he loved the old manners he illustrated by his admiration of the Turks, whom he spoke of with constant respect.

'They are the only good people in Europe, far honester than others individually, and lying about as much politically. Coming from Turkey to France is like passing from lions to lap-dogs : they alone of all nations have known how to manage the two only real means of happiness, energy and repose.'

And, in accordance with this feeling, he lamented continually the issue of the conflicts on the Loire, commonly called the Battle of Tours, as the greatest misfortune of the European world. ' The Saracens would have occupied France, have crossed to England, and even we English should have been gentlemen.' And thus, although the Republic was his ideal, in the whole range of his poems and ' Conversations ' there is not one word of apology for democratic licence, nor one whit less condemnation of the injustice or folly of the ruled than of the rulers ; it is his judgment of popular applause that

> The People never give such hearty shouts
> Saving for kings and blunders.

' Liberals,' he said, ' were Republicans as curs are dogs,' and ' the discovery that everybody who had made money was discontented cured me of Radicalism.' ' Tom Paine once said to me : '' The day will come when you will have as little reason to like England as I have, perhaps less, as you will have more to lose.'' '

In the matter of the affections there is less discrepancy between his writings and his life. If a

6

woman could have forborne, and swayed herself according to the vacillations of his temper, his whole character might have been modified, and his happiness saved in his own despite.   It was a kind of pride with him that all children loved him.   In his demeanour to his own his tenderness was excessive.   That his boy of thirteen had not ceased to caress him, is spoken of as a delight he could not forego by sending him to England even under the care of the scholar he most respected, Dr. Arnold—unmindful of his own fine words :—

> The worst
> Of orphanage, the cruellest of frauds,
> Stint of his education, while he played
> Nor fancied he would want it.

He was always drawing analogies between children and flowers ; and there was no mere fancy in the well-known lines—-

> And 'tis and ever was my wish and way
> To let all flowers live freely, and all die
> Whene'er their genius bids their soul depart,
> Among their kindred in their native place.
> I never pluck the rose ; the violet's head
> Hath shaken with my breath upon its bank
> And not reproached me ; the ever-sacred cup
> Of the pure lily hath between my hands
> Felt safe, unsoiled, nor lost one grain of gold.

In his garden he would bend over the hand the with a sort of worship, but rarely touched one the them.

' I remember,' he wrote to Southey in 1811, ' a little privet which I planted when I was about six years old, and which I considered the next of kin to me after my mother and elder sister. Whenever I returned from school or college, for the attachment was not stifled in that sink, I felt something like uneasiness till I had seen and measured it.'

The form which the notoriety of this sentiment took in the Florentine legend was that he had one day, after an imperfect dinner, thrown the cook out of the window, and, while the man was writhing with a broken limb, ejaculated, ' Good God ! I forgot the violets.'

I fully agree with Mr. Forster in regarding those latter years of his residence at Florence as the brightest, at any rate the least clouded, of his life. It was at that time (in 1833) that our acquaintance began, through an introduction from Mr. Julius Hare, my tutor at Cambridge. I was seized with the fever of the country, and Mr. Landor took me into his villa, where I spent several most happy weeks in a daily enjoyment of his rich mind

woman or discourse.   The diligent exercise of composition had been most useful to his mental temperament, and his physical health was excellent.
' I have no ailments,' he said to me ; ' but why
should I ?   I have eaten well-prepared food ;   I
have drunk light subacid wines and three glasses
instead of ten ;   I have liked modest better than
immodest women, and I have never tried to make
a shilling in the world.'   He professed to care for
no compliment and to be molested by no criticism,
yet it evidently pleased him that his writings were
loved by the men whose opinions he most esteemed,
and enjoyed by a small but competent audience
beyond.   At that time his domesticity, though not
cheerful, was not angry ;   his children were still in
bud and flower ;   his few relations with residents
in the city friendly without familiarity ;   and the
pilgrimage of literary sight-seers sufficient for the
variety of life without any unseemly intrusion. His
house was sufficiently spacious for the climate, and
all the more so from the absence in the rooms of
all that he called ' carpentry,' which he especially
disliked. The English notion of *comfort* was odious
to him.   ' There is something,' he said, ' smothering
in the very word—it takes the air from about one.'
Even mirrors and lustres he eschewed as only fit

for inns, if not magnificent.　On the other hand the decorations of Art were abundant, and it was the habit of the place to look upon him as the victim of the ingenious imposture which fills so many English galleries with the fictions of great pictorial names.　No doubt his overweening positiveness served him as ill here as elsewhere, and he would refer anyone who doubted his ' Raphael ' or his ' Correggio ' rather to the hospital of St. Luke in London than to the Academy of San Luca at Bologna.　But it is to be remembered that Italy at that time had not been so thoroughly ransacked as now, and that Landor anticipated the public taste in the admiration of the painters of the early Italian schools.　Thus, amid some pretenders to high birth and dignity, his walls presented a genuine and most goodly company of such masters as Masaccio, Ghirlandajo, Gozzoli, Filippo Lippi, and, native to the place, Fra Angelico.　I wrote some verses on this subject about that time, which he pleasantly acknowledged, saying—' They show you have been in Greece after being in Germany.' I insert them here rather as a memorial of our intercourse than for any merit of their own.

TO WALTER SAVAGE LANDOR.

AGED NINE YEARS.

Sweet, serious child,—strange boy !   I fain would know
  Why, when I fondly talk and sport with thee,
I never miss th' exuberant heart-flow
  Which is the especial charm of infancy :
Thou art so wise, so sober,—nothing wild,—
I hardly think, yet feel, thou art a child.

For had th' unnatural bondage of a school
  Checked the fair freedom of thy vernal years,
Encumbered thy light wings with vulgar rule,
  And dimmed the blossoms in thy cheeks with tears,—
Thou mightst have been as grave, as still, as now,
But not with that calm smile, that placid brow.

Nor has the knowledge of dull manly things,
  And intellect grown ripe before its time,
Defiled thy being's freshly-salient springs,
  And made thee conscious of a world of crime ;—
With all thy earnest looks, as spirit-free
As ever infant dancing down the lea.

Is it not that within thee, as a shrine,
  The power of uncommunicable Art
Is working out its ministry divine,
  Silently moulding thy all-virgin heart
To its own solemn ends?   Thus dost thou wear
That priestly aspect,—that religious air.

And every circumstance of outward life
  Tends this sublime ordainment to unfold ;
Is not each chamber of thy dwelling rife
  With miracles of purest painters old,—
The Saints and Patriarchs of Art,—who knew
How best to make the Beautiful the True?

Thou hast them all for teachers ;—He is there,
　The limner cowled, who never moved his hand
Till he had steeped his inmost soul in prayer :
　Him thou art bound to in a special band,
For he was born, and fed his heart, as thou
On storied Fiesole's fair-folded brow.

There thou canst read, with deeper reverence still
　Rare lessons from the later monk, who took
The world with awe of his inspired skill,
　To which the Apostle leaning on his book,
And those three marvels in old Lucca shown,
Bear witness, in the days we call our own. *

There too Masaccio's grandly plain design,—
　Quaint Ghirlandajo,—and the mighty pair,
Master and pupil, who must ever shine
　Consociate Sovereigns—thy preceptors are ;
Now pass him by, who with grave lines looks down
Upon thee, Michel of the triple crown.

Thou hast a Sire, whose full-experienced eye
　Keeps harmony with an unerring heart,—
Who, of that glorified society,
　To thy young sense can every depth impart.
How dare I then deny thy perfect joy ?
How dare *I* judge thee, thou unearthly Boy ?

Looking forward to his later years, it is worth notice that a sale of his pictures which took place at Manchester, and the contents of which were severely criticised, in no way represented the value of his collection. It comprised a large number of inferior pieces, such as he was continually picking

---

* Fra Bartolomeo.

up for his own amusement, and many of which he distributed among his friends; several, no doubt, baptized with higher names than they deserved. The fine works of which he was justly proud, and in the contemplation of which he found constant delight, still remain in the possession of his family.

Who that heard can forget the amusing and instructive comments with which he exhibited his treasures? for instance :—

'Look at Andrea's truculent-faced Madonnas and Holy Children that seem ready to fly at you.'

'Velasquez not only painted better horses than anyone else, but made his men ride better.'

'See there the pictorial grace quite independent of the gracefulness of the forms represented.'

'The Bolognese school are glorious in landscape —what a pity they tried anything else.'

His dearest companion, however, was always his Dog—a love which lasted till the very last. His desolation at the loss of ' Pomero, mi Pomero,' the ' caro figlio' with which he used in his old age almost to gambol down Catherine Place in Bath, making it ring with bark and laughter, is recorded in lines which will be inscribed on many garden-tombs of departed favourites.

O urna ! nunquam sis tuo eruta hortulo :
Hoc intus est fidele—nam cor est canis.
Vale, hortule ! æternumque, Pomero, vale.
Sed, si datur, nostri memor.

I do not remember which was the 'Pomero' at
that particular time, but it was a daily pastime to
take him between his knees and converse with him
in such language as, 'Ah ! if Lord Grey (or any
other notoriety of the hour) had a thousandth part
of your sense, how different would be things in
England !' He scouted the notion of fear of dogs,
saying, 'When a dog flies at you, reason with it,'
and 'remember how well-behaved the Molossian
dogs were when Ulysses sat down in the midst of
them as an equal.'

His repugnance to common relations with mankind showed itself in a peculiar way with respect
to the pleasures of the table, in which he took an
unreserved enjoyment; his highest luxury was
dining alone, and with little light, and he would
often resort to Florence for that purpose. He
said 'a spider was a gentleman—he eat his fly in
secret.' But this dislike to conviviality did not at
all prevent him from performing agreeably the
duties of host, and the repast was ever seasoned
with valuable talk. He liked open discussion, but

6*

within decorous limits. 'I enjoy no society,' he said, 'that makes too free with God or the ladies.'

His trenchant opinions on subjects of literature were always explicable by some reference to his own habits of thought and lines of knowledge. Latin was so thoroughly familiar to him that his judgments on the classics were like those of a contemporary. With Ovid he was completely content, but there was something that displeased him in both Virgil and Horace; 'they were excellent,' he said, 'for school-boys and school-masters:' but they did not write Latin. I suppose he meant his ideal of what the language ought to have been. When a style really captivated him, there was no exaggeration too large for its praise—Herodotus, Demosthenes, and Catullus in the old world, Voltaire and La Fontaine in the modern, were the only perfect masters, 'but there is something above perfection—such as Shakspeare.' Of our own popular writers he was rarely laudatory.

'Roscoe's works are one feather-bed of words;' 'Gibbon is an old dressed-up fop, keeping up the same sneering grin from one end of his history to the other with incredible fixity;' 'Young, in his snip-snap verse, is as sure to destroy a poetical thought he has got hold of as a child a butterfly;'

'In Hallam you may light on a small cake of fine flour, but the rest is chaff, chaff.' 'Walter Scott's verse is not to be sung or danced—it is to be jumped.' But in a letter to Mr. Crabb Robinson, he designates Southey, Coleridge, and Wordsworth as 'three turrets, none of which could fall without injuring the others.' Again, 'Southey's translation of the "Cid" is all written in words sanctified, not corroded, by Time'—was one of many praises of his friend's various productions. He rarely persisted in his harsher judgments. Of Byron, in an early 'Conversation,' he had drawn a clever fictitious portrait —'strong as poison, and original as sin;' and he never liked him till after his heroic death, for so we may call it in spite of Goethe's solemn judgment—

> 'Till, from all earthly fetters free,
>   He strove to win the Hero's lot;
> But Fate decreed that must not be,
>   And murmured 'Thou hast earned it not.' *

Shelley he had refused to know from some private reasons, which he afterwards passionately regretted, and always wrote and spoke of him with infinite respect. Of Keats he felt that 'time only was wanting to complete a poet who already sur-

* Vide 'Euphorion's Song' in the second part of *Faust.*

passed all his contemporaries in this country in
the poet's most subtle attributes.' To Walter
Scott he was more than specially harsh, calling him
a 'great ale-house writer;' but in later days he
fell back on the Novels with more than enjoyment,
and wondered that Englishmen did not glory in
them more: 'The Germans would, and so should
we, if hatred of our neighbour were not the religion
of authors, and warfare the practice of borderers.'
Of the Brothers Smith he candidly avowed, 'I
ought especially to hate Bobus and Sydney for
licking me out and out, Bobus in Latin poetry and
Sydney in English prose; but Bobus has had no
rival in Latin this 1800 years.' (Lord Dudley
ranked the Latin poets—Lucretius, Bobus, Virgil.)
I could give many examples of the rare and generous delight with which Landor ever welcomed
the apparition of Genius; it was as a fresh metal
to the mineralogist, as a new planet to the astrono-
mer; the ardour was sometimes excessive, but
often more than justified by the event, and those
who are now received with the trumpets and
shawms of popularity look back with deeper gratitude to the prescient praise of the young-hearted
veteran who decorated them from the laurels and
myrtles of his own classic garden. So was it to

the very last—to the Boy-poet, who shortly before his death,

> '—came as one whose thoughts half linger,
>   Half run before—
> The youngest to the oldest singer
>   That England bore,—'

and took away the affectionate benediction of his predecessor in the noble art of keeping alive in high British culture the form and spirit of ancient song.[*]

Landor moved little from Florence; once to Rome with Julius Hare, once to Naples with Lord Blessington, and in 1832 to England. One can well picture him in the Vatican before the silent presences of history, uttering:

> Vos nudo capite atque vos saluto,
> Qui saltem estis imagines proborum,
> Ne, multis patria procul diebus,
> Oblitus male moris usitati,
> Viso quolibet aut probo aut amico,
> Dicar rusticus ad meos reversus.

At Naples he met his old competitor in politics and learning, now relaxing himself in Italian composition, the author of the once famous, now forgotten, 'Pursuits of Literature;'' and on a sultry

[*] Vide Swinburne's *Poems and Ballads.*

day, with the *Pifferari* blowing under the window,
thus greeted him :—

> The Piper's music fills the street,
> The Piper's music makes the heat
> Hotter by ten degrees :
> Hand us a Sonnet, dear Mathias,
> Hand us a Sonnet, cool and dry as
> Your very best, and we shall freeze.

In England he had a most courteous reception,
not only from fashionable people turned radicals,
which amused him highly, but from Charles Lamb
at Enfield, Coleridge at Highgate, and ' dear Julius
Hare' at Cambridge.   The last he saw for the first
time, and their three days' intercourse made an
epoch in each existence.   Then to the Lakes, and
to Southey, his devotee, and with a passing
visit to Wordsworth (who, he thought, meant to
hit him a double blow, by a remark, ' That Prose
will bear a great deal more of Poetry than Poetry
will of Prose ') to his friends at Warwick.   That
once great town, he found, was joining its own
noises to those of Leamington, which, he remarks,
' is almost all built on a property that I only
escaped the encumbrance of by a single life.'
Julius Hare and Dr. Worsley, the present Master of
Downing College, accompanied him on his return

to the Villa Gherardesca. There is an interesting passage connected with this journey in the Memorials of the Hare family, in which Augustus replies to some objection made to Julius' companionship with his heterogeneous friend: ' I cannot regret that he should travel with Landor, though I do regret the abuse I hear of the latter. I wish that I could speak publicly in defence of a man whose heart I know to be so large and overflowing; though much of the water, from not having the branch which Moses would have shown him thrown into it, has unhappily been made bitter by circumstances. But when the stream gushes forth from his natural affections, it is sweet and plentiful, and as strong almost as a mill-stream. For his love partakes of the violence of his character; and when he gives it a free course, there is enough of it to fill a dozen such hearts as belong to the ordinary man of pleasure, and man of money, and man of philosophy, and to set the upper and nether mill-stones in them a-working.'

I need not detail the miserable domestic tumults that ended in his self-banishment in 1835. Before that period he had written the 'Examination of Shakspeare,' of which Charles Lamb said, ' That only two men could have written it—he who did

write it, and the man it was written on.'   There is
no gentler verse in the language than the ' Scrap
found in Willy's Pocket,'—no grander counsel
than this ever given to the young, rich and poor :—

' Young gentlemen, let not the highest of you
who hear me this evening be led into the delusion,
for such it is, that the founder of his family was
originally a greater or better man than the lowest
here.   He willed it and became it; he must have
stood low ; he must have worked hard, and with
tools, moreover, of his own invention and fashion-
ing ; he warned and whistled off ten thousand
strong and importunate temptations—he dashed
the dice-box from the jewelled hand of Chance, the
cup from Pleasure's, and trod under foot the sor-
ceries of each ; he ascended steadily the precipices
of Danger, and looked down with intrepidity from
the summit ; he overcame Arrogance with Sedate-
ness, he seized by the horn and overleaped low
Violence, and he fairly swung Fortune round.   The
very high cannot rise much higher ; the very low
may : the truly great must have done it.   This is
not the doctrine of the silkenly and lawnly religious : it wears the coarse texture of the fisherman,
and walks uprightly and straightforward under it.'

The story too of the Youth who failed at college,

and died broken-hearted on the banks of the Cher-
well—'literarum quæsivit gloriam, invenit Dei,' is
unsurpassed in the beauty of pathos.   This was
followed by the letters of Pericles and Aspasia, a
book well described by an American critic as one
'that we are frequently forced to drop, and surrender ourselves to the musings and memories, soft
or sad, which its words awaken and cause to pass
before the mind.'   Its pages take you to the theatre
where 'Prometheus' is played, to the house where
Socrates and Aristophanes meet, to the promise of
the youth Thucydides, and to the Statesman who
dies, 'remembering in the fulness of my heart, that
Athens confided her glory and Aspasia her happiness to me.'

These 'Epistles' are a treasure-house of fine
apothegms : one, on the duty of the historian as
distinguished from that of the archæologist, is worth
recording in reference to the novel treatment of the
matter in our days :—

'We might as well in a drama place the actors
behind the scenes as in a history put valiant men
back, and protrude ourselves with husky disputa-
tions. Show me rather how great projects were
executed, great advantages gained, and great
calamities averted. Show me the generals and the

statesmen who stood foremost, that I may bend to
them in reverence—tell me their names that I may
repeat them to my children. Teach me whence
laws were introduced, upon what foundation laid,
by what custody guarded, in what inner keep preserved. Let the books of the Treasury lie closed
as religiously as the Sibyl's : leave Weights and
Measures in the market-place, Commerce in the
harbour, the Arts in the light they love, Philosophy
in the shade ; place History on her rightful throne,
and, at the sides of her, Eloquence and War.'

Goethe somewhere says ' that the monument of a
man should be always his own image,' and Landor,
enlarging on this theme, insists that it should be
only a bust and a name. ' If the name alone is in-
sufficient to illustrate the bust, let them both perish.'
Yet no one more than Landor has shown, by his
own incisive epitaphs, the power and the duty of
fit memorial inscriptions : they are in truth the best
securities for historical fame, and even in their vul-
garer forms transmit to the gratitude of posterity
services and examples which it is too much to expect the mere name to suggest and record. Latin
is no doubt the fit lapidary language, but when in
English can be composed such inscriptions as that
of Lord Macaulay on Sir Thomas Metcalfe, or that

of Landor on Southey, it may well be the vehicle for the commemoration even of the greatest men.

Landor's exile in England, for such it strictly may be termed, was passed chiefly at Bath, the scene of his wilful and wayward youth ; he loved that graceful town and was fond of comparing it with Florence. In the hospitable and intelligent society of Gore House he had a London home, and a constant literary activity occupied his time and sustained his spirits. The 'Dialogues on Dante,' which he entitled the ' Pentameron,' were criticised in the ' British and Foreign Review ; ' and in Landor's unpublished ' Reply,' written under the false impression that Mr. Hallam was the author of the article, there is an interesting summary of his estimate of his own literary worth, and a curious deprecation of the common judgment of the foibles and limitations of his genius. Perhaps as years had gone by and carried with them the choice adherents of his name and fame, he had fallen back on some hopes of a broader though lower level of recognition. So certainly it became with the intimacies of his private life ; the circle of his acquaintances was no longer confined to those who knew how to manage and elude, or who for love's sake endured, the susceptibilities of his peculiar temperament. Hence strong likings suddenly changed into hatred and disgust; hence uncontrollable passion at deceptions and self-deceptions; hence wild literary revenge for supposed social injuries; hence the acts which the indiscriminating judgment of Law might not excuse, but which the Press and Public might have regarded with some consideration for a life so honest and a heart so high.

Of the sad six years of his final return to Italy there is one bright portion in the summer he passed at Siena in a cottage hired for him by Mr. Robert Browning—'the kind friend,' he writes, 'whom I had seen only three or four times in my life, yet who made me the voluntary offer of what money I wanted, and who insists on managing my affairs here and paying for my lodgings and sustenance.' He also resided in the family of Mr. Story, the eminent American Sculptor, who declares, as Mr. Browning records, 'that his visit has been one unalloyed delight to them, and this quite as much from his gentlemanliness and simple habits, and evident readiness to be pleased with the least attention, as from his conversation, which would be attractive under any circumstances. He may be managed with the greatest ease by civility alone.' To some en-quiry respecting his deficient sleep he replied, ' I ought not to complain. I shall very soon sleep twenty-four hours out of the twenty-four.'

Landor continued his composition in verse almost to the very end. In the last 'Conversation' he wrote, Andrew Marvel felicitates Henry Marten with having met with Oliver Cromwell and con-versed with John Milton : 'Believe me, it is some-what to have lived in fellowship with the truly great and to have eschewed the falsely.' This Landor had ever done, and if Antipathy had been the presiding genius of his life, the reason assuredly was, that he demanded from all men his own no-bility of mind, in addition to all the qualities of temper and wisdom which he never forgave himself for not possessing.

Happy, indeed, should I be to extend in any degree the knowledge and use of Landor's writ-ings ; I say advisedly the use, because though often surprised that they are not more the objects of literary delectation and amusement, I still more regret the neglect of their obvious utility as ex-amples of English composition. His style is so natural an outgrowth of a rich imaginative mind, and so clear a representation of thought, that its study is not likely to lead to any servile imitation, while it conveys the most distinct impression of the

charm and power of Form.   Abounding in strong,
even passionate diction, it is never vague or con-
vulsive ; magniloquent as declamation can demand, it is never pompous or turgid ; humorous
throughout, it avoids contortion and abhors caricature.   In strange contradiction to the temper of the
writer, its chief characteristic is self-command, and
it bears a weight or paradox with as much ease
and dignity as ordinary writing its lightest commonplace.   Though not alien to the treatment of
modern life, it is undoubtedly most at home in the
old world ; and in such ' Conversations ' as those
of Lucullus and Cæsar, Epictetus and Seneca,
Epicurus and the Grecian maidens, Marcus Tullius
and Quinctus Cicero, and in the ' Epistles ' of Pericles and Aspasia, there is a sense of fitness of language that suggests the desire to see them restored,
as it were, to the original tongues.   Not only, indeed, would passages from these works be the best
conceivable objects of translation in any classical
examination, but versions of them, by competent
scholars, might well be applied, as has been proposed with the ' Dialogues of Erasmus,' to the
purpose of early instruction in Latin, and alle-
viate the difficulty in which all teachers of schools,
at any rate, are placed by the absence of any

original writings in that language which combine interest of subject with the facility of construction and purity of style required in an instrument of linguistic education.

For the greater part of his English verse I cannot expect more than the sympathy and admiration of poets. The imagination of the reader is too often necessary to supplement that of the writer to make his poems popular even with those who are capable of appreciating their sentiment and imagery. But what may be pressed upon the public judiciously and with every hope of success by the lovers of Landor's fame, are such smaller pieces as were inserted in the first issue of Mr. Locker's pleasant little volume of ' Lyræ Elegantiarum,' and unfortunately suppressed as an infringement of copyright. They are the very perfection of poetic epigram—real flowers of harmonious thoughts. They dwell on the memory like combinations of certain notes of music with circumstances of life, and seem to me to be the equals in that form of literature best treated by Goethe and Voltaire.

It is certain that Landor prided himself on his Latin more than on his English writings ; and I am glad to append some remarks on his style and diction by the most venerated of living English scholars.

'Landor undoubtedly possessed a command of the Latin language which enabled him to use it for every purpose, and to adapt it to every theme, from the fables of Greek mythology to the incidents and characters of his own day. It is not easy to convey a notion either of the merits or of the faults of his Latin poetry to those who cannot judge of it for themselves. Its character cannot be illustrated by a comparison with any other Latin poetry, ancient or modern. Its style is not that of either the golden or the silver, or of any earlier or later age of Latinity. It is the style of Landor, and it is marked with the stamp not only of his intellect, but of his personal idiosyncrasy. This is the cause of that obscurity which must be felt, even by scholars, to mar to some extent the enjoyment of his Latin poetry. He was perfectly able to write in a style transparent as that of Ovid. But such was not his pleasure. He despised popularity; he disdained imitation; he abhorred all that savoured of mannerism, conventionality, and commonplace. He aimed at independence, originality; at the quality for which Mr. Matthew Arnold has endeavoured to naturalise, in English literature, the French word *distinction;* and thus it happened that when he might have clothed his thoughts in clear, simple, and natural language, he preferred forms of expression in which the stone is often too hard for common readers to get at the kernel. Nevertheless there are in these poems passages of exquisite tenderness and pathos, and others which display an extraordinary power of word-painting. No doubt the author's poetical faculty is more largely developed in the longer compositions; but the shorter are more deeply impressed with the signature of the man; not, indeed, always in the most winning aspect, or the gentlest mood of inspiration. Now and then harmlessly playful, but much oftener instinct with the bitterest sarcasm; keen and poisoned shafts, levelled sometimes at the objects of his political animosity, sometimes at persons from whom he believed himself to have suffered a private wrong. If it may be said that he set any model before himself, it must have been Catullus. But neither the Idyllia Hæroica, nor Gebirus, nor Ulysses in Argiripa, approach the Atys or the Epithalamium. The Hendecasyllabi recall not unfrequently the poet of Sermio.'

I have engraved the portrait by Mr. Robert

7

Faulkner, preferring it to the frontispieces in Mr.
Forster's volumes. The first, indeed, is interesting,
as indicating in the boy the unboyish contemplation and premature self-absorption that developed
itself so fatally to his happiness ; but there is no
trace of the sweetness and humour of the mouth
which redeemed the anti-social character of the
upper features. The second is as unsatisfactory as
engravings not of, but from, paintings usually are,
and Mr. Boxall's work is seen at a great disad-
vantage. Mr. Landor died in September 1864,
aged eighty-nine, in his favourite Florence, but
not upon that famous Hill to which his name has
given one more illustration. His family still re-
side in the Villa of his love, which many a future
pilgrim of letters will visit with reverence and gratitude.

V.

THE BERRYS.

THE question of the man-about-town : 'Who
are those Miss Berrys who have been running all
over Europe ever since the time of Louis Qua-
torze ?' has been fully answered in the three portly
volumes compiled from the diaries, letters, and
memoranda left by Miss Mary Berry to the care of
the late Sir Frankland Lewis, to be used by him
for biographical and literary purposes, as he might
think fit.   He died without any such publication,
and they came into the hands of Sir George Cornewall Lewis, the scholar, critic, and statesman, whose
loss friends and country have deeply deplored.
His well-instructed and accomplished widow, Lady
Theresa Lewis, undertook the vicarious work, and
within a few weeks of its appearance she too passed
away, soon followed by her brother Lord Clarendon, leaving Mr. Charles Villiers at the present
time the only living representative of a numerous
generation of an historic and intellectual race.

This record of busy death stands strangely side by side with the one long life, of which Lady Theresa's book is the narrative, a life that nearly lasted its century, and which included within its observation as memorable a period of our world's history as the sun's light has ever shone upon.   There is something in these occasional long spaces of individual existence which seems to make them especially favourable vehicles for biographical narrative ; the one figure standing by the protracted course of the stream of time concentrates round itself the images and interests of the past, and acquires an integral value which at any one moment of its being it would hardly have seemed to have possessed : it becomes identified with even more than its own experiences, and is judged not so much by what it was as by what it might have been.

Memoirs therefore such as these do not require the justification of any rare superiority of talent or character, and will be read with pleasure by many on whom the personage whose name they bear leaves little or no impression.   There are others, on the contrary, who might desire a more distinct representation of Miss Berry's personality ; but they may remember that Biography is no easier than Life ; and that, while every one has attempted

to contemplate his own mortal existence and that
of others, each as a co-ordinate whole, with its
special character, its individual meaning, its exceptional moral,—he has been constantly foiled by his
inability to comprehend all the fragments before
him, and compelled to content himself either with
a vague delineation which he leaves to be filled up
by other thoughts and other experiences, or by a
work of art which he knows to be the child and
creature of his own imagination. When Plutarch
placed in noble array for the contemplation of ages
to come his images of heroes and sages, or when
Dr. Johnson drew that gallery of poets, so many
of whom only survive in his portraiture, the writers
must have been conscious how little of the real
men lay behind those strong or graceful representations, how much that was even faithfully recorded may convey a false impression, how much
was inevitably omitted which might contradict
every deduction and alter every estimate. Thus,
in these latter days of literature, while we are more
and more thirsting for what is most true in humanity, and ever widening our interests in the
adventures and vicissitudes of mankind, we receive
unwillingly those biographies in which the artist is
predominant, even when agreeably and skilfully

executed; and we are very indulgent with any congeries of materials out of which we can ourselves embody some living personality, which, either for its own sake or by its contingencies and surroundings, challenges our attention or regard. Yet I should like, from the motley contents of this book, as well as from my own recollections and some private sources, to draw a more or less living portraiture of the lady whom our generation mainly remembers as the centre of a most pleasant social circle, and to trace by what combination of circumstances and character she came to live an almost public life without forfeiting or infringing the conditions of a simple and unostentatious existence, and to die amid the affectionate regrets of the foremost men of our own day, after having been courted by Horace Walpole and having refused to be introduced to Dr. Johnson. There always seems something patriarchal in relation to ourselves in persons who have lived to the present generation from before the French Revolution. That deluge has left a strait behind it, separating the historical worlds, and those who have been on the other side of it seem to have enjoyed a double life. Miss Berry's youth witnessed the great century of common sense, and the chief era of the liberation of

the human mind, closing in an *auto-da-fè* of political fanaticism, which still affects the imagination of
mankind: she was the living tradition of a world
of shattered hopes, dispersed allusions, and drifted
philosophies.

The personal circumstances of her girlhood were
singularly unpropitious. To the daily troubles of
genteel poverty was added the continuous gloom
of a domestic disappointment, her father having
been at one time the supposed heir of a wealthy
Scotch uncle, and afterwards supplanted by a more
active and less scrupulous brother. Of her mother
she had one glimmering infantine recollection, a
pale figure in a green dress, who had left little
other remembrance in the family than that she had
often prayed that her children might be endowed
with a vigorous character, an aspiration which in
Mary's case was undoubtedly accomplished. The
father could not impart to this desolate home
either useful occupation or pleasant companionship;
and the young ladies do not seem to have enjoyed
any advantages of instruction beyond the most ordinary teaching of their class in that not very intellectual time. When Mr. Berry first settled in
Yorkshire, Lady Percy, who lived at the neighbour-
ing great house at Stanwick, formed a kind of

friendship with his wife ; but this was not continued to the daughters, nor would it have been of much use if it had been, for the lady was soon after divorced on account of her intimacy with a Mr. Bird.

Occasional visits to their cousins, the Cayleys, a family which for many generations has borne, and still bears, a stamp of much talent and originality, seem to have been the only opportunities either for cultivation of intellect or development of character afforded to them; and yet, by the time when an increase of income, consequent on the uncle's death, enabled them to make a tour on the Continent, they were not only sufficiently well-informed to enjoy fully all the novelties and associations of travel, but so distinguished by their manners and conversation, combined with much personal beauty, that they were at once admitted to the best company, wherever they might find themselves, and laid the foundation of the social popularity they were destined to enjoy so long. A sufficient command of the Latin classics to give a scholarly turn to their knowledge, without a taint of pedantry ; a familiarity with the French tongue, which throughout life made the society of foreigners as easy to them as that of their countrymen ; a thorough understanding of their own language and literature, as exhibited in its best and purest models, which shone in all their conversation, and enabled them in mature years to express themselves on paper in a forcible, judicious, and graceful style ; an adequate study of the principles of Art, combined with a fair facility of practice —these were the results of the self-culture which the Misses Berry acquired in a remote provincial home, and which they might well have regarded through the long vista of years, not with the bitter remembrances of toil, effort, and privation, but with a legitimate pride in the conquests of talents and will over adverse fortunes, and with a grateful consciousness of the mental faculties that could do so much for themselves, and needed so little obligation to others.

The journal of this her first foreign tour, in 1783, which such a young woman might write, must naturally be intended for her own pleasure and reference, or, at most, for the perusal of intimate friends ; and the reproduction of it, at something more than eighty years' interval, has just the interest of the distance of time and nothing more. There are names there fresh which this generation can just remember,—such as M. de Staël consulting her on his marriage with Mdlle. Necker ; there are incidents of hard travel over paths now level or

7*

familiar—such as the journey to Chamouni on four planks under a canvas roof; there are some few traces of old-world manners,—such as the ballets at the Neapolitan theatre, where the Queen appeared on the stage in the character of Ceres and the Kings of Naples and Sweden as Lapland hunters pursuing their courtiers disguised as bears,—which are curious to recall: but, on the whole, it will hardly hold out its place even in that not altogether unamusing literature—Old Travels.

Two years after their return to England the Berry family took a house on Twickenham Common —a most important incident in their destiny—for in the autumn of 1788, at the house of Lady Herries, wife of the banker in St. James's Street, they were introduced to Mr. Horace Walpole, the finest of fine gentlemen and fine writers, the prince and patriarch of Dilettanti, the reviver of supposed Gothic architecture, and the lineal representative of one of the greatest of English names. The first night he met them he avoided their acquaintance with a characteristic reserve: he had heard so much in their praise, that he concluded they must be all pretence; but the second time, in a very small company, he sat by Mary, and found her ' an angel inside and out.' He soon did not know which sister he liked best, except that ' Mary's face was formed for a sentimental novel, but ten times fitter for a fifty times better thing—genteel comedy.' He could give her no higher praise—Genteel Comedy was the ideal of his life ; and from that day to the close of it he acted the part of the veteran friend and paternal lover to both, with tact, with tenderness, and with fidelity.

It is impossible to overrate the value of this association to the Misses Berry's social position, though its influence on their character and pursuits may have been exaggerated. It established and fixed them as personages of the best English society ; it gave them all his numerous circle of acquaintances out of which to make their friends, and by its very delicacy and difficulty it exercised and made manifest those sterling qualities of generosity and discretion which underlaid their more prominent attractions.

To Horace Walpole himself this relation was at once a true intellectual pleasure, and the familiarity of these ladies with Continental literature and manners made their intimacy especially agreeable to the correspondent of Sir Horace Mann and the adorer of Madame du Deffand, while their peculiar

freedom from petty prejudice or feminine folly enabled him to repeat to youth and beauty the compliment he loved to address to the blind and aged
object of his affectionate admiration. 'Sit down
there, Good Sense!' Miss Berry evidently shared
many of his literary prejudices, as for example, his
dislike of Dr. Johnson, whom she would not know.
'He would have said something disagreeable of
my friends, and we should have insulted each
other.' He found, too, in this sisterhood an
ingenious means of expressing the warmth of his
attachment, which saved him from the position
of an aged wooer, and either lady from the imputation of an interested connection. They were
his 'twin wives.' 'I pique myself,' he writes, on
the day of their departure for the Continent in 1790,
'on no other philosophy but what a long use and
knowledge of the world has given me—the philosophy of indifference to most persons and events.
I do pique myself on not being ridiculous at this
very late period of my life; but when there is not
a grain of passion in my affection for you two, and
when you both have the good sense not to be displeased at my telling you so (though I hope you
would have despised me for the contrary), I am not
ashamed to say that your loss is heavy to me.' Not

that the suspicions of a scandalous public were altogether eluded, for a newspaper paragraph, soon after his succession to the earldom and an additional estate, having ill-naturedly connected his name with that of his *protégée*, aroused an amount of indignation hardly commensurate with the offence. In an eloquent letter (October 1791) Miss Berry's pride reverts to the hereditary injustice which cast its shades over her early life, and she candidly tells him that 'If our seeking your society is supposed by those ignorant of its value to be with some view beyond its enjoyment, and our situation represented as one which will aid the belief of this to a mean and interested world, I shall think we have perpetual reason to regret the only circumstance in our lives that could be called fortunate.' These expressions, and the whole tenour of Miss Berry's conduct, combined with a circumstance to which we will presently allude, seem to negative the notion prevalent amongst her friends—that she voluntarily declined the advantages of fortune and position which she might have enjoyed as Lord Orford's wife; although there was a prevalent story that the Duchess of Gloucester frequently asked him, ' When am I to call Miss Berry my aunt?' and that his invariable answer was, ' Whenever Miss Berry pleases.' There is no trace in her papers of any proposal of the kind, and there was in him a sensitive dislike of all rash and exceptional behaviour, and an absence of all sturdy independence of the opinion of the world in which he moved, that would have naturally disinclined him to such a step, except as an alternative of some great annoyance. If the question had been before him, whether he would lose altogether the society of these dear young women or try to obtain one of them as his wife, he would probably have hesitated ; but this supposition in itself implies some state of circumstances which never existed, and a change of character on the part of either of the sisters, which would have destroyed their moral identity. With all his courtesy and kindness to Agnes, it is impossible not to see that Lord Orford beheld her with a reflected light, and it is no disparagement to her memory that, by herself, she was not likely to have acted on his imagination or fixed his affections as Mary did, and, in a lesser degree, Agnes through Mary. And Mary, before she had known Horace Walpole, had already met with the man who had inspired her with a profound and lasting passion, whom she idealised with a womanly desire that belied her wonted sense and led astray her sober judgment, and whose infidelity and desertion were almost more than even her proud and firm nature could sustain.

From an isolated sentence in Miss Berry's diary of the year 1818, it appears that some passages of affection had taken place between her and the Lord Fitzwilliam who bequeathed his noble collections to the University of Cambridge. When visiting the Museum she recognised his old valet, who told her that his master had frequently spoken of her to him, and she adds, 'What a difference in our two fates had they been united! It seems to me that he might, perhaps, have gained as much as I should; but who knows?' With this exception, there is no allusion in the whole of her journals to the question of marriage, except in the one romance of her life —her engagement to General O'Hara. This name occurs in the first part of her expeditions to Italy, May 30, 1789. 'With M. Ronconi, M. Conway, and General O'Hara, to the upper parts of St. Peter's.' During the next twelve years, as far as these records go, we know nothing of the relation between them, except from some slight allusion in Lord Orford's letters. He tells her in 1790 that some one is appointed Lieutenant-Governor of Gibraltar in the place of her friend, General

O'Hara, and adds, he shall be sorry if he is mortified, and she consequently. In the same strain the
next year he writes, ' O'Hara is come to town, and
you will love him better than ever ; he persuaded
the captain of the ship, whom you will love for
being persuaded, to stop at Lisbon, that he might
see Mrs. Damer. He has been shockingly treated.'
And again, ' I have seen O'Hara, with his face as
ruddy and black and his teeth as white as ever,
and as fond of you too, and as grieved at your fall
as anybody—but I. He has joined a better regiment.' In 1793, ' Our friend O'Hara is recently
made Governor of Toulon ; ' and late in the same
year, ' O'Hara is arrived at Toulon, and, if it can be
preserved, he will keep it.' He was then wounded
and taken prisoner, and on his liberation in 1795
he joined the Berrys at Cheltenham, and Lord
Orford writes, ' I am delighted that you have got
O'Hara. How he must feel his felicity in being at
liberty to rove about as much as he likes : still, I
shall not admire his volatility if he quits you soon ; '
adding at another date, ' Yes, here is your letter,
and I like all it tells me, that you have chained
your General to your car ; ' language which almost
sounds as if he was fully aware of what was going
on then between them, for about that time General

O'Hara and Miss Berry were formally engaged. In the following year O'Hara was appointed Governor of Gibraltar, and proposed an immediate marriage, in order that she might accompany him; but she conceived it to be her duty to decline this offer out of consideration for others. 'In submitting to this choice,' she wrote, 'I think I am doing right. I am sure I am consulting the peace and happiness of those about me, and not my own.' It is believed that this self-sacrifice was made in relation to an attachment which had sprung up between her sister Agnes and Mr. Ferguson, of Raith, the son of the man in whose favour her father had been disinherited, and which it was feared might receive a check by the change in Mary's condition. If this is so, the issue was doubly painful. General O'Hara, under other influences, which, it is said, accompanied him to his post, broke off the engagement he had contracted, and after some years the affections of the younger sister were blighted by a similar destiny.

This was the event of her life, against the effects of which she was ever striving with a brave spirit, but which lasted to the very end. In the June of 1796 she writes to an intimate friend :—

'Do not suppose this long period of mental and bodily suffering has been lost upon me. I have communed much with myself in my own chamber, I have reflected, and seriously reflected, that, however little I have hitherto enjoyed and much I have suffered in life from the circumstances in which I have been placed being quite inappropriate in my situation, still that a being endowed by nature with a sound understanding, possessing a cultivated mind, and a warmly affectionate heart, cannot be intended for unhappiness,—nay, can never be permanently unhappy but for its own fault; and that, with a conscience as clear as mine, it will indeed be my own fault if I do not make my future life less uncomfortable than my past.'

Again, in December :—

' After a twelvemonth passed in the most painful, agitating, and unavoidable suspense, I find myself not only totally disappointed in a plan of happiness, founded on the most moderate desires, and pursued by the most rational means, but obliged to change my opinion of one of the characters in the world of which I had ever thought the highest, and in whose known truth and affection I have even had the most entire confidence and the sincerest satisfaction long before I considered him in any other light than that of a friend. I shall not dwell on the effect which you will easily guess all this must have had on a heart as warm and as *little generally* confiding as mine, but a heart which, when once it trusts, trusts ƚo implicitly.'

But when his character is attacked by some one else, with a charming feminine inconsistency and latent passion, she writes :—

' Mr. L., you say, observes that my affections have been more deeply engaged than I was aware of, and Mrs. D. has repeatedly intimated the same to you. Needed you any intimation that my affections *must* have been *deeply* engaged before I resolved, or even thought of marrying ? Had I even chosen to think of making what is called a *prudent* marriage, did you suppose, that I, in common with all my sex, might not have done it ? or could you suppose *this* a *prudent* marriage ? Did my silence on this subject deceive you ? And did you really believe me capable of the *platitude* of talking in raptures, or enlarging on the character and perfections of the man whom I considered as my husband ? Now that he no longer stands in that position, it is not *my* having reason to complain of him that shall prevent my doing him justice. I know not where you have taken your reports of his character, but I know that a character " universally highly thought of" is the last I should choose for any intimate connexion, for (except in early youth) nothing but mediocrity can possibly attain it. I have heard O. H. called too *exigeant* and *worriting* by idle officers under his command, and too bold by the ministerial people here, after the failure at Toulon ; but in my life I never heard an allegation against either his heart or his understanding ; and if I had, I should not have believed it, because in a long acquaintance I have myself *known* and *seen* repeated proofs of the excellence of both. Instead of not knowing " any real virtues he possesses " until this unfortunate affair, in which I am still convinced his head and not his heart is to blame, I know nobody whose character united so many manly virtues. It was this, joined to a knowledge of his conduct in all the relations of life in which he then stood, that entitled him to the " approbation and love of such a heart " as mine, and I felt and know he decidedly " suited me as a friend," because to an excellent understanding, great natural quickness, and much knowledge of the world, he joined an affectionate tenderness of heart which had always inspired me with a degree of confidence and inti-macy you have often heard me say I hardly *ever* felt with *any* other person. . . . I still believe that had this separation never taken place, I should never have had to complain of him, nor he to doubt me.'

It is impossible not to feel some interest in the career and character of the man who inspired this passion and earned this regard, and we have in the excellent novel entitled 'Cyril Thornton,' by Colonel Hamilton, the portrait of him in his later years, vividly sketched by an eyewitness, and, it would seem, his personal friend. He is described as being then at the age of sixty-seven remarkably handsome, and giving the impression of a man who had been distinguished both in camp and court :—

' He was a bachelor, and had always been noted as a gay man—too gay a man, perhaps, to have ever thought of narrowing his liberty by the imposition of the trammels of wedlock; notwithstanding an office of considerable emolument which he held, I believe, in the Royal Household, he had dissipated his private fortune and become deeply involved in his circumstances. He was a *bon vivant*, an amiable boon companion—one to whom society was as necessary as the air he breathed ; at his own table, in nothing distinguished from those around him, except by being undoubtedly the gayest and most agreeable person in the company. Anecdote-telling was at once his forte and his foible—his forte, because he did it well—his foible, for, sooth to say, he was sometimes given to carry it into something of excess.   He would entertain his friends by the hour with the scandalous title-tattle that had been circulated at Court or in the clubhouses some thirty years before, and did more than hint at his own *bonnes fortunes* among the cele-brated beauties of the British Court, and the *bona-robas* of France, Italy, and Spain.   I have seldom heard a finer voice or one more skilfully managed.'

From this sketch it is not difficult to imagine a reverse of the medal equally true.   There were friends of Miss Berry who thought she had had a good escape from a noisy roystering Irishman, with little taste in literature, and who probably would have ended as a domestic martinet and a social bore.   But it was not for her to understand this; and when, in 1802, some one entering the opera-box of Lady Stuart, at Paris, mentioned that the Governor of Gibraltar was dead, Miss Berry fell motionless to the floor.   Death held sacred the memory that life had cherished, and thus she writes to Mrs. Cholmley, in 1805 :—

'. . . . . I must tell you that yesterday driving out with Lady Douglas I told her my *whole story*. She had often expressed such a wish to be informed

of some *particular chapters*, as she called them, before she began reading *my Life*, that I thought it
unfriendly, indeed had no wish, to withhold it.
Luckily I spoke to a person disposed to enter into
my views, and my sentiments for the subject of my
tale. She had heard much of *him* from the Duchess
of Buccleuch, with whose brother, Lord Mount-
shannon, he was particularly intimate. She had seen
him once or twice with Lady Pembroke, was delighted with him herself, and so was everybody she
knew. Nobody could enter more into my feelings,
think higher of my conduct, or be more astonished
at *his*, which I could only end by saying, remained
to this day as inexplicable to you and to me as it
could be to her. She had heard something of it
indistinctly before from Lady Louisa Stuart; and
the other day, at dinner here, a gentleman happen-
ing to mention a now intended attack upon Cadiz
from Gibraltar, which he said had been proposed
by O'Hara, and was always *his* plan, the effect she
saw it had upon me, made her feel herself growing
red and pale every instant from fright that he
should again mention the subject. I was not quite
well, and the mention of that plan brought forcibly
to my mind the flattering idea with which O'Hara
accompanied it, when he first mentioned to me

having proposed such a plan to Government, that, after a brilliant success in an action of *éclat*, I should be the less blamed for becoming his! Though I had no pain, but rather satisfaction in talking over all this yesterday with Lady Douglas, yet it brought all the circumstances, all the scenes, all the feeling of that twelvemonth so strongly before me, that I have been living ever since in reverie with *him* and with *you*.   Where else, alas! can I ever meet with company so exactly suited to my head and my heart!'

Again, to Mrs. Damer in 1811 :—

' I was at Park Place yesterday.   It had rained much in the night, and was a gray, damp, melancholy day, suiting well with the feelings I carried to it.   Never did I see a place which, without being much altered, is so perfectly changed, so *triste*, so comfortless!   Everything is neglected: the seats all falling to pieces, the trees overgrown in some places, and in others dead and left standing, the poor little flower-garden with its fountain dry and its borders flowerless, its little arcades overgrown and broken and the thorn-tree in the middle let to spread over the whole space.   Oh, how every step of it affected me!   I saw you and O'Hara sitting under this thorn-tree in its trim

days, and myself having left you merely to enjoy
the delicious sensation of knowing you were expressing for me every sentiment that I could wish
to inspire. I saw him following me into the laurel
walk, and in giving me a letter (which I had acci-
dentally dropped) in a joking manner, first con-
vincing me of the seriousness of the sentiment I
had inspired. I sat down at the end of the library,
and saw your form at the bottom, on a ladder,
arranging the new-placed books, and the look you
gave and recalled, when you found us sitting at
the other end of the room, just where you had left
us when you returned again to your work. . . I
am so glad I have seen Park Place *once*, in spite of
all the melancholy it inspired, but I should be sorry
to see more of it.'

Once more, forty-eight years after the breach of
his plighted faith, Miss Berry reopened the packet
of letters that had passed between them, and, as
Lady Theresa Lewis well expresses it, 'attached
to it the following touching little record of the
disappointed hopes and blighted affection that
deepened the natural turn of sadness in her character' :—

' His parcel of letters relates to the six happiest
months of my long and insignificant existence,

8

although these six months were accompanied by fatiguing and unavoidable uncertainty, and by the absence of everything that could constitute present enjoyment. But I looked forward to a future existence which I had felt, for the first time, would have called out all the powers of my mind and all the warmest feelings of my heart, and should have been supported by one who, but for the cruel absence which separated us, would never have for a moment doubted that we should have materially contributed to each other's happiness. These prospects served even to pass cheerfully a long winter of delays and uncertainty, by keeping my mind firmly riveted on their accomplishment. A concatenation of unfortunate circumstances—the political state of Europe making absence a necessity, and even frequent communication impossible, letters lost and delayed, all certainty of meeting more difficult, questions unanswered, doubts unsatisfied. All these circumstances combined in the most unlucky manner crushed the fair fabric of my happiness, not at one fell shock, but by the slow mining misery of loss of confidence, of unmerited complaints, of finding by degrees misunderstandings, and the firm rock of mutual confidence crumbling under my feet, while my bosom for long could not banish a hope that all might yet be set right. And so it would, had we even met for twenty-four hours. But he remained at his government at Gibraltar till his death, in 1802. And I, forty-two years afterwards, on opening these papers, which had been sealed up ever since, receive the conviction that some feelings are indelible.'—M. B., October 1844.

In the year following this great desertion the Misses Berry lost their distinguished friend, and whom in the classic sense they would have gladly named patron—Horace Walpole. In Mary's journal these words only, underlined, record the loss—*Lord Orford dies.* Henceforward the two sisters had to face life together and alone. Their kindly father almost inverted the due relation between them, and was a real encumbrance on, though an interest in, their existence. Their favourite distraction, travel, was no longer possible—they were shut up within the four seas. In 1798 Miss Berry writes :—

" Most thoroughly do I begin to feel the want of that *shake out* of English ways, English whims, and English prejudices, which nothing but leaving England gives one. After a residence of four or five years we all begin to forget the existence of

the continent of Europe, till we touch it again with
our feet. The whole world to me, that is to say,
the whole circle of my ideas, begins to be confined
between North Audley Street and Twickenham.
I know no great men but Pitt and Fox, no King
and Queen but George and Charlotte, no town but
London. All the other Cities, and Courts, and
great men of the world *may* be very good sorts of
places and of people for aught we know or care ;
except they are coming to invade us we think no
more of them than of the inhabitants of another
planet. We should like, indeed, just to know
what is become of Buonaparte, because we are
afraid of our settlements in India, and because we
are all great newsmongers and politicians, though
more ignorant, more incapable of any general view
upon these subjects, than any other people with
whom I ever conversed, the French of ten years
ago only excepted.'

No wonder, then, that she was eager to avail
herself of the negotiations at Amiens, and one of
her first remarks is the great improvement of the
country in cultivation and apparent prosperity
since her former visit. The Revolution, indeed,
fell with very unequal severity on different portions
of France, and the cooler temperament of the

Northern population not only checked the violences of political fanaticism, but enabled them to use the advantages which the destruction of the old order of things placed within their grasp. This journal is the best description I have seen of the short truce which Western Europe then enjoyed, and the sketches of social life in Paris are distinct and interesting. Towards the First Consul himself Miss Berry was far from feeling that odd mixture of contempt and terror that possessed the English mind for so long in their estimation of a character that still exercises the conflicting judgments of mankind. Not that she thought otherwise than the ordinary society of her day of the French people and their Revolution, though she may have protested against her friend Walpole coupling Tom Paine and Dr. Priestley—the 'trull Sillery' and the 'virago Barbauld'—in a common condemnation. But in the beginning of 1800 she had written, ' What think you of the *man Buonaparte*, absolute King of France, quietly established in the Tuileries ! For my part I admire him, and think, if he can keep his place, he does his country a service. . . . Now that an absolutely aristocratical government is established, what is it to us whether Louis

Capet or Louis Buonaparte' (a prophetic slip of the pen, indeed!) 'is at its head. If the nation is once in a state to maintain the relations of peace and the conditions of treaties, what *have* we, what *ought* we to have to do with the means?'

The first time she beheld Napoleon was at a grand review, where she only notices his good seat on horseback, his sallow complexion, his very serious countenance and cropped hair. When she saw him nearer, the man of the Court Circle seemed very different from the man of the Parade: he appeared taller, and with an uncommon sweetness in his look, his whole countenance giving rather the impression of complacence and quiet intelligence than of any decided penetration or strong expression whatever. His eyes seemed light grey, and he looked full in the face the person to whom he was speaking. It may be in reference to this appearance that there occurs in the diary an elaborate analysis of the connection between the colour of the eyes and mental character, commencing, 'Pale grey eyes with dark hair belong to all the very extraordinary characters I have seen—Buonaparte, Byron, &c.; while dark eyes with the greenish cast imply the first rank with regard to the qualities of the heart and the second with regard to intellect;

while dark eyes with the reddish cast, however fine, with dark hair, indicate no superiority either of the mind or the affections.' Madame de Staël received her in a loose spencer with a bare neck ; and no signs appear of the earnest friendship which afterwards grew up between them. She was, of course, delighted with the treasures of the Louvre, but remarks with justice how much many of them had suffered from those restorations of which every traveller to Madrid now sees the painful effects in the *Perla* and the *Spasimo.* In the Pantheon she speaks of seeing the ' tomb, or rather the cenotaph ' of Voltaire. It would be curious to know on what authority she makes the distinction, the discovery of the absence of the bones, which had been transferred there with so much pomp during the Revolution, having caused, within the last few years, much inquiry and controversy.

Returning to England after this singular visit, the Berrys crossed the Channel again in October for a lengthened tour, described in the same clear-sighted way as the sojourn at Paris, and with some amusing personal adventure, but, on the whole, not so well worth recording. There is one passage detailing all the discomfort of a night passed at Tourves, a village between Aix and Nice, and the strange way in which all that was painful in the recollection was dissipated and overcome by the delight of an early morning walk on the rocky edge of the Mediterranean, in the mild freshness of the southern winter air, with the sun rising out of the glorious sea, and the vivid green of the pines on the nearer hills, that will forcibly remind the reader of that beautiful page of Miss Martineau's 'Life in the Sick-room,' in which, leaving the bed and sickroom that seemed full of pain, she looks through the window-curtain on the flood of rays flashing over the waters, strewing them with diamonds, then gilding the green down below, then lighting up the yellow sands of the opposite shore to Tynemouth harbour, with the garden below glittering with dew, and buzzing with early bees and butterflies. 'I was suffering too much,' adds the invalid, 'to enjoy this picture at the moment; but how was it at the end of the year? The pains of all these hours were annihilated—as completely vanished as if they had never been—while the momentary peep behind the window-curtain made me possessor of this radiant picture for evermore.' . . . .

Miss Berry was struck with the unfavourable effect of the French Revolution and French inter-

course on the Swiss character: 'The peasants, I
believe, have really gained by the abolition of the
feudal and seigneurial rights ; but the inhabitants of
the towns, who were formerly an industrious, sober,
and (for the age they lived in) simple set of people,
are grown at once idle, insolent, and corrupted,
which sits infinitely worse upon the dull *grossiereté*
of the Swiss character than upon the pert *légèreté*
of the French.' The party, indeed, had soon after
to make their escape from Switzerland on the re-
newal of hostilities, which they did with difficulty,
not knowing how far the rigorous detention of
English travellers by the French Government
might extend,—the French influence at that time
being so dominant in that country that Miss Berry
speaks of the annexation of the Pays de Vaud to
France as a political certainty. She found little
gratification in returning to Lausanne, after an
absence of nearly nineteen years, which, she writes,
she had 'left while in the heyday of life, with a
thousand brilliant prospects, hopes, and ideas before one, all cruelly failed in a *manquée* existence,
and which at sober forty can never be revived.' It
was in this spirit that, in the following year, which
was additionally saddened by the final failure of
Agnes's engagement with Mr. Fergusson, which,

8*

besides the personal attachment, would have re-habilitated the sisterhood, as it were, in the family possession of which they always fancied themselves defrauded, she wrote an imaginary epitaph on herself, little thinking that forty-eight years would elapse before she laid down to her final rest : —

> Beneath this stone is deposited
> The dust of one whom,
> Remarkable for personal beauty,
> Considerable superiority of intellect,
> Singular quickness of the senses,
> And the noblest endowments of the heart,
> Neither distinguished, served, nor
> Rendered happy.
> She was
> Admired and neglected,
> Beloved and mistaken,
> Respected and insignificant.
> She endured years of a useless existence,
> Of which the happiest moment was that
> In which her spirit returned to the bosom
> Of an Almighty and Merciful
> Creator.

This sad summary of life and character will seem to many so incongruous with the successful woman of society, the cheerful host, the welcome guest, the friend and correspondent of so many important literary and political personages, and the intelligent observer of the fortunes of mankind, that they may

attribute many of its expressions to a morbid sensi-
tiveness or womanly affectation. But to those who
know her well it will appear just and true. Its
mournfulness might indeed, in some degree, be
attributed to a physical depression, to which she
was subject to an extent that the published portions
of her 'Journal' do not adequately represent, and
to what is called a melancholy disposition; but the
spirit of it is in accordance with all the graver mo-
ments of her life, and the temperament can hardly
be called melancholy, which avoided no occasion
of gaiety and no opportunities of healthy excitement. Nor was there a trait of sentimentality
about her: it was the habit of the time in which
she lived to treat emotions of that kind as very
well for the artistic conceptions of Florian, Gessner,
or Sterne, but as incompatible with the dignified
transactions of life and ridiculous in its manifesta-
tion. Indeed, the impression which Miss Berry
made on some of her acquaintances was that of
a rather hard than tender nature; and Lady Charlotte Bury, in her amusing and unscrupulous
'Diary,' accuses her of want of sympathy, and sac-
rificing her gentler feelings to her love of the
world—though, she adds, ' it must be said to her

honour that that sacrifice is never of kindness of heart or integrity of character.' *

It was in truth the serious consideration of the vague and fragmentary conditions of human life, under its best aspects, that gave to her mind at once its gloom and its solidity. One chief disappointment naturally gathered round itself the floating atoms of dissatisfaction, and she imaged them as its consequence and production—but no circumstances would have altered her view of the world, unless indeed some uncongenial companionship had degraded her perceptions and damaged her intelligence. Her relations to General O'Hara had perhaps more of female instincts about them than she avowed to herself, and though, when their novelty was past, she might have enjoyed a deeper personal happiness and contentment than it was her lot to obtain, she would never have been light in her judgments, or frivolous in her estimates of mankind.

And it was the same with the feeling of her own unimportance. It is with no mere vanity that she writes—

'Nobody ever suffered insignificance more unwillingly than myself. Nobody ever took more

* Vide Diary, vol. i. p. 88.

pains by every honourable means compatible with
a proud mind to avoid it. But it has been thrust
upon me by inevitable circumstances, and all I
have for it is to endeavour to forget myself and
make others remember how little I deserve it.'

This sense of injustice she would have resented
in the case of any other person as intensely as in
her own. Hence, without any vituperation of the
wrongs of women, she more than once betrays her
earnest consciousness of what she would have been
and done, with the liberties and opportunities of
manhood, and to her latest years she certainly
showed something masculine in her demeanour.
She never gave up the useful and sensible fashion
of distinguishing her male friends from her acquaintances by using their surnames, a custom now
nearly extinct in the higher circles of society, and
there was an occasional vigour in her expressions
of indignation which a puritan or purist might object to, but which had an antique flavour of sincerity
about it that quite compensated for the incongruity of the speaker and the phrase. Her complaints
of the subordinate position of her sex were of no
fanciful character. That their education (if education it can be called) is nearly ended at the very
time when their minds first open and are eager

for information and that the education of men begins ; that their reading is desultory and heterogeneous; that the endowments of what is called
a *woman-of-business* are those which would not
distinguish a lawyer's clerk, and which every
woman should be ashamed of not having acquired
—these seemed to her just grounds for discontent;
and when she adds that, with these disadvantages,
' it is a wonder that they are not more ignorant,
more perverse, and weaker than they are, and that
the wrongs and neglects which women of superior
intellect almost invariably receive from men are
revenged by the various evils which men suffer
from the faults and frailties of their wives and
female friends,' few thinkers of our day will dis-
agree with her.

It must also be remembered that much self-
regret and secret disappointment find a vent and
consolation in the speculative modes of thought
and various views of the external and internal
world that now occupy the attention of reflective
and educated persons. The *femme incomprise* of
our time, as well as the unappreciated man of
genius, have their metaphysical comforts, which
the hard realists of the eighteenth century knew
nothing about, or which, when they tried to use

them, they converted, like Rousseau, into poisons
and enchantments. When people were mystical
in those days they gave themselves up to devotion,
and made no attempt to mix up their imaginativeness with public life; when they were philanthropic they established foundling hospitals, or
taught the deaf and dumb to communicate with
the world; but they did not trouble themselves
with the elevation of the lower orders of society,
or the salvation of the whole human race. When
women wished to exert power or obtain wealth,
they ministered to the pleasures of the other
sex, and made capital out of their foibles and
their vanities; and the career of any one who
wished to gratify at once her ambition and her
virtue was by no means easy. It was, however,
very possible to retain by a certain *prestige* much
that they had won, when the means of acquirement
had themselves passed away, and such personages
as Madame Geoffrin and Madame du Deffand, at a
very advanced age, had more social authority and
political influence than youth, beauty, and talent
together would command in this country. True,
as one of the thousand historians of the Revolution
has said, the ' *vieille femme* had been so completely
guillotined that she never appeared afterwards; '

and Napoleon Bonaparte called Madame de Staël a
phraseuse, and sent her out of the country ; but yet
Miss Berry felt conscious that she was of more
significance when in France than in England, and
her familiarity with foreign manners and literature
had thus a decided tendency to encourage both
distaste of a station that must have appeared
admirable and enviable to many less successful
courtiers and purveyors of society, and her aspirations after something higher and more permanent
than the daily gratifications of a fashionable existence or even the cordial intimacies of its most
worthy members.   In the intensity of this feeling
she sometimes rises even above the practical good
sense and generous intuitions which were the habits
of her mind, and approaches a philosophy very
different from that familiar to her age and personal
surroundings.   That she should value and expound
the political economy of Malthus with a prophetic
spirit that would have done honour to any statesman; that the Canonico Bandini should write that
he never doubted ' *quin lectissima et literarum
amantissima puella Maria Berry memoriam mei
quamvis absens firmam animo suo retineret;* ' that
Professor Playfair should correspond with her on
the merits of Condorcet; that Sir Uvedale Price

should consult her on the 'Theory of Visible Beauty;' that Madame de Staël should have thought her '*by far* the cleverest woman in England,'—these all are the natural concomitants of the *femme forte* of the beginning of our century, but rarely do we meet with such a sentence as this, written by her in a foreign tongue, perhaps from a sense of the secret solemnity of the thought :—

'Je touche quelquefois, en méditant le bout de l'aile de quelques grandes principes fondamentales, de quelques idées lumineuses que je me sens incapable de débrouiller, mais qu'il me semble une autre existence me révélera. Elles sont suggérées souvent par des livres dont les auteurs sont cependant cent piques au-dessus de les avoir conçues.'

When staying at Guy's Cliff in 1807 with her accomplished friend Mr. Greathead, Miss Berry was so gratified with the perusal of his journal, that she determined to keep one regularly herself. She had hitherto avoided doing so, because she felt ashamed of the use, or rather the no use, she made of her time, and of the miserable minute duties and vexations which at once occupied and corroded her mind. 'But now,' she writes, 'that no *future* remains to me, perhaps I may be encouraged to make the most of the

present by marking its rapid passage, and setting
before my eyes the folly of letting a day escape
without endeavouring at least to make the best I
can of it, and, above all, without making impossible
attempts to mend or alter anybody but myself.'
If this project had been carefully worked out we
should have had a record of almost historical value
from this acute and conscientious observer; but
though many volumes of notes remain, they rarely
form a continuous diary for any considerable time
together.   Many of the notices seem dotted
down merely for personal remembrance, and remarks of any real interest are few and far between.
I give these pathetic extracts as an interesting train
of thought spreading over many years.

' The stream of time seems now to carry me
along so rapidly, that I already approach the brink
of the great Ocean of Eternity into which that
stream is hurrying to lose itself.   I feel so near
disappearing with it that I fain would catch at
some idle weeds as my bark glides by, to mark my
passage.   Thus I wrote and felt five years ago, in
October 1804.   It was the last fainting struggle
at exertion.   The following is the record I find of
the state of my mind on the same subject last
year, October 1808.   How heartily do I and my

friends shake hands when we meet alone at night, after an evening passed in any sort of company— now alas! however agreeable that company may be, to *have been* in it is now, to me, much more enjoyable than being in it.'

'Solitude broken by a book, and reverie when I can indulge in it, are my real enjoyments. The rest is merely desirable to give a zest to these— and so life glides by me. I no longer make an attempt to mark its course, and aware of the extreme rapidity with which it passes, feel the consolation of knowing that I shall not long be oppressed even by the painful sense of my own insignificance.'

The period between the Peace of Amiens and the termination of the war was very favourable to good society in London. The best English had nowhere else to go to. There were no railroads to promote perpetual motion, and no penny-post to destroy the pleasures of correspondence. The Whigs, excluded from office, except during Mr. Fox's short reign, strove to find in social preponderance a compensation for political dignity. The Tories might dominate in certain apartments at Westminster, but the London Houses were theirs. In their societies there was all that luxurious life

could add to the pleasures of considerable aristocratic culture, and to the excitement of an Opposition headed for a considerable period by the heir
to the Crown. There was, besides, an Opposition
Court at Kensington, where the Princess of Wales
collected all the wits—whose interests did not lie in
another direction—and all the fashion she could
persuade to patronise her. The table-talk of such
a time, accurately rendered, would of itself be interesting and, commented upon by such an intelligence as Miss Berry's, most instructive. For in
all these circles she and her sister had acquaintances, and, in some of them, friends. An accidental meeting with Lady Georgiana Cavendish in
1799 resulted in a life-long intimacy, and connected
her by many ties of kindness and affection with
the genial families of Cavendish and Howard, from
the generation of the celebrated Duchess of Dev-
onshire, to that of the amiable Lord Carlisle, who
has prematurely closed his generous, blameless,
and honourable career.

The first, and disagreeable, impression which
Caroline Princess of Wales made on Miss Berry
turned to a deep pity for a person, who she says,
' in conversation was so lively, odd, and clever,
but who was without a grain of common sense, or

an ounce of ballast, to prevent high spirits and a
coarse mind, without any degree of moral taste,
from running away with her.' She was, besides,
thrown a good deal into the Princess's company by
the liking she contracted for Lady Charlotte Lindsay, Sir W. Gell, and Mr. Keppel Craven, who
formed part of the Royal household. The picture
here given of this poor woman's scatter-brained
cleverness, her comical diction (she swore she
would never be anybody's ' cats-paw,' and to the
last she always spoke of ' The Bill of Pains and
Spikalties '), and her flagrant imprudence of demeanour, leaves the conviction on the mind of the
reader that, under the most favourable circumstances, her position in this country must have been
false and miserable. Neither the public commis-
eration for her strange destiny, nor the disrepute
and ill-favour of her enemies, nor her own many
kindly and liberal qualities, availed anything
against her want of dignity, decorum, and self-re-
spect. She was said to be the only friend the
Prince had ; for she vindicated his conduct by her
presence wherever she showed herself. She had,
however, sense enough to feel the value of such a
friend and adviser as Miss Berry, and, till her last
departure from this country, she treated her with

much respect, and with all the affection of which
her poor nature was capable. There is a touching
glimpse too of the Princess Charlotte at fifteen,
with her face damaged by small-pox to an extent
rarely seen at the time among the higher classes,
but with an open, lively countenance, and well-cut,
expressive features, saying ' she was afraid of dark
and dismal stories,' and telling a good one herself—knowing all about Miss Berry with a royal
readiness—telling Sir W. Drummond to go on
with what he was saying, ' for she liked nothing so
much as politics,'—and leaving the impression of
an undirected intelligence and an undisciplined will.
How far the influence of so sagacious a partner in
life as Prince Leopold would have modified her
character must be a matter for conjecture, but the
Princess Lieven, in those interesting memoirs of
her time which it is to be hoped will not be entirely
lost to the world, mentions that the Regent had
said to her that ' the death of his daughter had
been a most fortunate event for this country : she
would have made a very bad Queen.'

The friends whom Miss Berry found or made in
this circle are prominent figures in her Memoirs and
in her life. She outlived them all, Lady Charlotte
Lindsay only preceding her by three years. This

lady has left a most agreeable remembrance on all who knew her. She was of the noble family of which Lord North is the political representative, and whom nature favoured rather in their talents than in their external appearance. She may, indeed, have been the very personage of the well-known anecdote of the luckless interrogator who tried to remedy the unconscious incivility of his remarks on the statesman's wife by still ruder strictures on the daughter. When she said a good thing —and she said many—her features crumpled into an expression of irresistible humour. She used to give an amusing account of her marriage, which took place, like most nuptials in high life in those days, in the drawing-room of her father's house: the clergyman brought no prayer-book, thinking there would be no difficulty in supplying him with one, but no such article was forthcoming in the house, and the only way of getting over the difficulty was to perform the marriage by memory: the clergyman, confused with the novelty of the situation, came frequently to a dead stop, and could only continue by the fragmentary reminiscences of the company; 'Somehow or other,' said Lady Charlotte, 'I do not think that I was ever rightly married at all.'—She said, she had 'sprained her ankle so often, and been always told that it was worse than breaking her leg, that she said, she had come to look on a broken leg as a positive advantage.'—In her later days when once complimented on looking very well, she replied, ' I dare say it's true, the bloom of ugliness is past.'—Her *jeux-de-mots* were felicitous.   On the elevation of some childless personage to the Peerage, she remarked that he was ' of the new Order, which seemed the popular one, not the Barons, but the Barrens.'—One day, coming late to dinner in the country, she excused herself by the ' macadamnable' state of the roads.—When the question happened to be asked whether ' Yes' or ' No' was the more important word ? ' " No," of course,' she said, ' for it often means " Yes," but " Yes" never means " No."'.—Her graphic letters and journal give a very fair account of the Queen's trial and the evidence on both sides, and are not, on the whole, very favourable to her Royal Mistress; but they clear up the current story to which Dr. Lushington's speech gave rise, that her husband had sold her letters to Sir John Copley, who brandished them in her face during her examination : she merely said, ' he cross-questioned her like a murderer at the Old Bailey.'

Sir William Gell and Mr. Keppel Craven

belonged to that class of scholarly dillettanti which
will soon be a subject for archæology in English society. M. About suggests somewhere that 'What
was a *salon?*' will shortly be a proper question for
a competitive examination in History; and the combination of the pleasant play of intellect on trivial
subjects with a sound and accurate scholastic
knowledge, of the wit of the moment with the
study of a life, of the enjoyment of letters as a
luxury with its encouragement as a duty, is nearly
extinct among us. Put Sir William Gell's
'Handbook of the Morea'—the matter-of-fact of
the driest traveller—side by side with his letters
rampant with nonsense and glowing with fun, and
you have a chimera of character which we should
hardly venture to portray in a novel. Things and
men must now be all and each in their proper
places; but it may happen that if we are desirous
of banishing Humour from all the walks of life
where we think him superfluous or intrusive, and
telling him to go home, he may take us at our
word more strictly than we intend, and we may
lose sight of him altogether. After a life of events
and travel, Sir William Gell found in Italy an
asylum for his talents, his tastes, and his gout.
The *Via Gellia* of Rome and the *Villa Gellia* of

9

Naples will mingle his name with the historical
associations of the ancient past, while, at the latter
city, his contemporaries, towards whom he acted
as a sort of classic Consul of the place, and the
natives, down to the donkey-boys who carried him
in a sort of palanquin through his Pompeian researches, and who occasionally let him fall from
laughter at his jokes, will often recall his cheering
voice among the noisy memories of Southern
Italy.

Of Mr. Jekyll the wit there is a curious notice
in the following note written in 1813, confirming
Miss Berry's strong sense of her early personal attractions and of the waste she had made of them.

' A passion of two hours and a half's duration (we
will not say how many years ago) cannot possibly
hope that its *vestigia* will help your memory to a
sort of promise you gave the other day to come on
Sunday evening round to North Audley Street.
This then is meant to refresh that memory. Would
it could do as much for the charms that silenced
you for two hours and a half of the last century ! '

After a short visit to England came another and
longer tour, of which the main incident is the death
of Mr. Berry at Genoa. By the side of his coffin
she exclaims, ' What a strange thing is this human

life, when one can neither enjoy it nor wish to quit it!' She writes to Madame de Staël, 'This death leaves us without a duty to fulfil towards the living generation, nor have we any tie with that which is to come.' They returned to England in the autumn of each year, but left it again the following summer.

These frequent sojourns abroad and abundant social intercourse had not prevented Miss Berry from at least attempting to make some figure in literature. Heinrich Heine says, every woman writes with one eye on her manuscript and with the other on some favourite man; but her first effort was one of gratitude and devotion to the memory of the friend she had lost. Her translation of a preface to the letters of Madame du Deffand was a generous vindication of a connection which had been the object of much comment and ridicule, and which she did her best to place in a reasonable and amiable light. This she was in a great degree enabled to do by her knowledge of the peculiar and personal elements of the French society of that period, in which she took almost a cognate interest, while at the same time she never lost sight of a higher standard of morality or attempted to palliate what was really vicious and

sensual about it.   It is the more important to keep
this in mind, because in her comedy of 'Fashionable
Friends,' which was acted with success in private,
but which failed on the stage, and still more in the
'Characters,' which she wrote after the manner of
'La Bruyère,' there is an undeniable coarseness of
manners and a very easy treatment of the moral-
ities of life.   A discrepancy in the handling of such
an imaginary subject which strikingly illustrates the
truth of Charles Lamb's Essay on the 'Artificial
Comedy of the last Century,' where he asserts
that Comedy has just as much right to a dramatic
interest, apart from moral deductions, as Tragedy,
and that you might as well be supposed to approve
of the murders of Macbeth or Othello, as of the
unreal imbroglios and elaborate seductions of the
Fainalls and the Mirabels, the Dorimant, and Lady
Touchwoods, the heartless fops, the faithless wives,
the rascally valets and the swindling chamber-
maids, because you enjoy the poetry of the one and
the wit of the other.   It was indeed a characteristic of the time in which Miss Berry lived, that a
lady of unblemished life and untainted mind should
take pleasure in such an exercise of her faculties, and
her best friends probably did not regret the public
failure of her dramatic enterprise, although it

received the direct sanction of a respectable Scotch professor, who augured its brilliant success. I have spoken of the ' Characters ' which Miss Berry amused herself in portraying, according to a literary fashion then prevalent. No specimen of these is given in Lady Theresa Lewis's memoir, and some refer to personages whose relatives are still upon the scene. The following judgment of the now historical Duchess of Gordon must be read with the same qualifications which we have applied to the Comedy, and it is curious as an illustration of manners, besides its own wit and liveliness.

' Flavia was intended for a woman of gallantry. Circumstances have settled her in the country, the wife of a dull husband and the mother of a dozen children. Her constitution and her conscience are eternally at war and will continue so, till age delivers her up to devotion and robs both of the victory. As a woman of gallantry she would have had every virtue but one, and all the others would have been easy to her. As a sober matron the practice of that one is so painful as to rob her of all satisfaction from any of the others. Made for pleasure, she would have had just enough senti-ment to enhance her favours, and too much constitution to allow her sentiment to tire any one with her constancy. True to one lover whilst he possessed her, if he contrived to throw another in her way, he might be always sure to get rid of her with only just as much distress as would flatter his vanity and interest the next man to whom she became attached. Too much occupied with herself and her desires to think much of other people, she would have been satisfied and benevolent to all the world except her rival, and the moment this rival ceased to offend her in that capacity, she would have been capable of making her her bosom friend. Her confessor would have cleared her conscience of all her daily transgressions, with less trouble than he now has to quiet her doubts about past wanderings and her regret at present mortification. Her naturally warm feeling would have repented on her knees to God with hardly less transport than she would have returned to sin in the arms of her lover. As a woman of gallantry she would have been the best of her tribe, and her vices would have been natural to her. As a matron, her faults only belonged to her, and her virtues are so little her own that they punish instead of making her happy.'

The following sketch of Lord Brougham in his

younger days will be interesting to those who now can judge how far its anticipations are correct. He had evidently in his rise in life come to take less notice of his former friends and they were making the best of it. It is dated 1808.

'I do more justice to Brougham than you imagine. I am aware that his present manner and habits do not proceed from his character but from circumstances—from his not being naturally placed in the situation which his ambition, his feelings, and his taste, equally make necessary to him, and which his intellect tells him is his due. His whole mind is so set on securing the means necessary for this purpose that everything and everybody who cannot in some manner help him, are neglected, or unnoticed, or indifferent to him. Above the mean arts of actual adulation to those he despises, he selects the best he can among those most fitted for his purpose, and consoles himself for the weaknesses his quickness must see, and his prudence not notice in their characters, by being doubly severe on the characters of others. When he shall have secured the independence and distinction to which his abilities in this country must soon raise him we shall see him more generally attentive to merit, less severe to the want of it, judging of persons as they really are, and not as they can or may be useful to him, and, above all, getting rid of a certain sort of affected reserve in his conversation, and of childish gravity in his behaviour. We shall see him acquiring an unaffected popular manner which may better make his superior talents be forgiven by the trifling and the dull. Playfair and Lord Webb Seymour both agree that he has had two or three different manners since he first appeared in the world, and the present is far the worst.'

Miss Berry's only serious literary production was the 'Comparative View of Social Life in France and England ; ' a book which has perhaps been superseded by the abundance of memoirs and *résumés* with which the press of late years has teemed, but which, taken in relation to the English information of that time on such subjects, exhibits much research and power of arrangement. Of the many and various judgments it contains, some are erroneous, and even superficial, but there is a discrimination and fairness in estimating the peculiarities and excellencies of the two countries, which produced as much effect in France as in England. Benjamin Constant said of the first volume, ' On vit avec les individus : ce n'est pas une lecture, mais une société dans laquelle on entre,' and he calls on her to complete her object (as she did in a certain degree in her second volume), by describing that new French nation, which at once overthrew and occupied the old social existence.

In this work, in her letters, in her journal, in her fragments, Miss Berry ever asserts her sense of the importance and value of Good Society for the happiness and civilisation of mankind. To her it was no mere pleasure or even grace of life, it assumed all the dimensions of a duty. After the decease of Mr. Berry, the ladies, though perhaps not more really independent, entered on a more distinct social position, remaining more habitually at home, and receiving their friends more regularly. The custom of entertaining your friends with nothing but tea and conversation had by this time become frequent and popular. The first lady of fashion who attempted it was Lady Galway, with the assistance of her daughter, the ' lively Miss Monckton' of Boswell (afterwards the celebrated Lady Cork), who used to boast that with nothing but Good Company she beat the Faro-table of Albinia Lady Buckinghamshire. * Contempora-

* Lady Galway was the second wife of the first Viscount. Her daughter Mary, born in 1750 and married in 1786 to the seventh Earl of Cork, only died in 1840.

9*

neous with Miss Berry were the *salons* of Miss
White, whose social spirit fought against the continual presence of a terrible malady, and of Lady
Davy, who came to London with the prestige of
having ruled over the Modern Athens.   All these
passed away, but year after year the Miss Berrys
remained in the full stream of London life, only as
time advanced they went out less and less, till
there were few evenings before the first of May
(when they always let their town-house and took
one in the suburbs) in which the lighted windows
did not beckon in the passing friend.   No serious
incident broke in on, or checked, this regular life of
sensible entertainment till the death of their cousin
Mr. Fergusson, whose generosity and hospitality
were almost all to them that the possession of
Raith would have been.   After that sorrow, their
society became more limited to intimates, and with
a trait of manners that recalled the old *régime*,
they never wore rouge again.   In the later years
the entries in the Diary become rarer and more
occasional; for long lapses of time they cease
altogether; every now and then there is a spasm
of the old regrets at not having been and having
done more in life, and we light on words pathetic
as these :—

'But why recall all this *now*, at my latest hour?
when, had all happened differently—had I been
called to show all that I myself am capable of, I
should be *now*, neither better nor worse. Perhaps
much worse than the poor, old, feeble soul, now
dictating these lines and blessing God for every day
that passes, with an absence of all acute pain of
body, and for every day that allows of that calm of
mind which ought to accompany a nearly approaching departure to another state of existence, under the
pitying eye of an all merciful and all just Creator.'

My last extract will be strange in its serious
imaginativeness, and a strong instance how one
sorrow re-acts upon others.

A DREAM.

I THOUGHT that in one of the finest summer
evenings of the South of Europe, after having been
driving in an open carriage as far as a road overlooking the Mediterranean allowed, on our return
towards the lines of the fortress we got out to
walk, while such a moon as is only to be seen in
the South of Europe was rising in the clear blue
heavens. After a few steps I exclaimed, 'What an
exquisite scene! and how exquisitely is my mind
attuned to enjoy it? For you must be aware, my

dear soul, said I, pressing the arm of her on whom
I leant, that all your intentions, all your plans for
my happiness, have more than succeeded. That
I am more gratified, more happy, more satisfied
with *his* passion for me than I could have imagined
—more proud of the change of opinion I have
given him of my sex, and of the entire confidence
he has now in me. Let me add too, more pleased
with my situation and the duties it entails on me.
I need not say that the comfort, the support, the
repose, the increase of easy enjoyment that I receive from your friendship, leaves not a chink of
my heart unoccupied. I have now only to pray
that I may be removed from the world, before this
beautiful vision of life fades, as fade it must, from
my senses. I sometimes see *his* lively countenance and gay mind, looking with a sort of anxiety
at my grave composure, and your enquiring eye
cast on me. But happiness is a serious thing, and
mine, (as Champfort says) "ne s'appuie pas sur
l'illusion, mais repose sur la vérité." I have sometimes fancied during this last month, that I might
be going to give him a child. I want not this new
interest, every chink of my heart, as I have said,
is filled up. But perhaps a child of mine might
be an interest to you in your later life and a

support to him in old age. If so, it shall be welcome, provided that then I may be allowed to depart. I can in all confidence leave my child in *his* and *your* protection, and shall die convinced that I have exhausted everything that can make life desirable.' .˙. .

Here I awoke with my eyes suffused with tears, to find myself a poor, feeble, old soul never having possessed either husband or child, and having long survived *that* friend who my waking, as well as my sleeping thoughts, always recall to me, as the comfort and support of nearly thirty years of my sadly insignificant existence.

———————

That this should have been written in 1840, about the time I was most familiar with the social circle in Curzon Street, and when I should have instanced Miss Berry as a model of brilliant and blithe old age is humiliating to my penetration, but nothing new to psychology. Indeed, I never well understand her saying to me what surprised me at the time, 'Every woman should run the risks of marriage who could do so: the dusty highway of life is the right road after all.'

It only remains to me to close these views of the worth of these ladies, and their career by a few general observations on the social characteristics of the country and generation in which their lot was cast, and the relations to them in which they stood. When Madame de Chevreuse said she had no disinclination to die, *parce qu'elle allait causer avec tous ses amis en l'autre monde*, when Count Pozzo di Borgo in some English house drew a newly-arrived foreigner into a corner, with the eager request, *Viens donc causer, je n'ai pas causé pour quinze jours.*'—they expressed that *esprit de sociabilité*, which, Madame de Staël said, existed in France from the highest to the lowest, and which in this country is so rare, that it not only gives to those who exhibit it a peculiar and foreign manner, but easily subjects them to the imputation of frivolity or impertinence. The universal reticence of all men in high political station with us, quite justifies the remark of a traveller that ' An Englishman refuses to speak just in proportion as he has anything to say;' and there is, no doubt, more adventure related and more mutual interest excited in any French *café militaire* than in the United Service Club, where there is hardly a man present, who has not been the witness of, or the actor in, some of the historical events or memorable circumstances of our age.

Neither our language nor our temperament favour that sympathetic intercourse, where the feature and the gesture are as active as the voice, and in which the pleasure does not so much consist in the thing communicated as in the act of communication; and still less are we inclined to value and cultivate that true Art of Conversation, that rapid counter-play and vivid exercise of combined intelligences, which bears to the best ordinary speech the relation that serious Whist bears to 'playing cards,' and which pre-supposes, not previous study, but the long and due preparation of the imagination and the intellect.

It follows that with us the conversationist is rather looked upon with curiosity and interest as a man endowed with a special gift, than accepted as an acquisition to the social commerce of life. In listening to the philosophical monologues of Coleridge, the illustrated anecdotes and fanciful sallies of Sydney Smith, the rich outpourings of Lord Macaulay's infinite knowledge, or the picturesque and prophetic utterances of Mr. Carlyle, we have been conscious that we were rather enjoying a substitute for good conversation than additions to the common stock. The monopoly of attention which was required, was, in most cases,

willingly conceded ; but even the wonderful intellectual exhibition did not make up for the deficiency in that sympathy between the speaker and
the hearers which gives a relish to very ordinary
parlance and very inferior wit, and which heightens
tenfold the enjoyment of the communication of
brighter and loftier ideas.

It is noticeable that certain English persons, notwithstanding the impediments of the language,
produce more effect in conversation with foreigners
than with their own countrymen.   We suspect this
must, to some extent, have been the case with Miss
Berry, to have elicited such warm expressions of
admiration from Madame de Staël, who attached
special importance to that faculty, and to have
made all visitors from the Continent so thoroughly
at home in her *salon.* Good nature and good
sense were really all that could be predicated
of the substance of her usual talk, but in the
manner of it there was a cheerful appreciation of all
that was said or done, which gave encouragement
to the shiest—an appeal to any wit or wisdom
the room might hold to come out and show itself,
which was rarely unheard,—and a simplicity which
dispersed by its contact all insolence or assumption.
Add to this the knowledge and the interest

acquired by an acute observation, and a retentive memory through this unusually long and varied life, and you have a combination all the more agreeable from its absence of the marvellous or the sublime. The greater part of the frequenters of Miss Berry's society might think themselves at least as clever and well-read as she was; and, though they were probably mistaken, they did not go away with less self-satisfaction. The conversation at Lydia White's might have been more literary, and at Lady Davy's more scientific, but at the Miss Berry's it had a flavour of fashion about it, which is not distasteful even to the most philosophic or matter-of-fact Englishman, and kept itself totally free from any speciality which could be made an object of ridicule or ground of offence. By its very familiarity and kindliness, this society was liable to the invasion of the garrulous and the tiresome; but even the specimens of that inevitable species which were found there were more tolerable than in houses of greater pretence, and became inspired by the genius of the place with some sense of mercy or of shame.

From the multitudinous shape which London society is now assuming, two consequences are imminent; first the difficulty of large re-unions, agreeable because in so vast a multitude there must be somebody whom you wish to meet, from the un‐fitness or inability of our houses to contain the whole of one's acquaintance, and secondly, the retirement within a very limited circle of relatives and private friends of those persons who would have been willing in the old time to have contributed their fair share to the social enjoyment of others. With the excuse of real discomfort abroad, joined to an Englishman's natural inclinations to stay at home; with the difficulty of meeting the few he likes, added to the certainty of encountering a crowd he abhors; with the increasing severity of the duties and respon‐sibilities of public life, and the diminution of the external respect and importance it imparts, there is every inducement to our wealthier, and nobler, and more fastidious countrymen to retain an exclusiveness of habits and an isolation of life, which can be indulged in with impunity by Legiti‐mists in Paris or Men-of-letters in Boston, but which, if systematically persisted in, will here seriously impair the due relation of classes, and alter the political structure of our civil existence. The great can no longer remain in an empyrean of their own, even if that atmosphere be purer, wiser, and better than the world below; but, as unfortunately it is the tendency of all exclusiveness of this kind to generate a very different kind of atmosphere, there is the double peril of the injury to the order and the damage to the individuals. It is, therefore, no exaggeration to say, that such a society as the Misses Berry established and maintained for nearly half a century—bringing together on a common ground of female intercourse, not only men illustrious in different walks of life, but what might aptly be called the men of the day—men who had won and men who were winning, men who wished to learn and men ready to teach, restrained and softened by a womanly influence that never degenerated into the social police which a less skilful hostess often finds necessary to impose—had its moral and political bearings, besides its personal and superficial influences.

This then is the real meaning and right of such persons to respect and remembrance. Inexplicable sympathies underlie all human association, and are the foundation of the civil order of the world. That men should care for one another at all, thought Mohammed, is always a mystery; and it is just in proportion that they care for one another, so as to take an interest in one another's daily life, that society is harmonised, and, beyond

Mohammed, christianised. Honour, then, to the good old ladies, who helped on this good work! They will soon be only personally remembered by those to whom the streets of London have become a range of inhabited tombs; yet the day may be distant before social tradition forgets the house in Curzon Street where dwelt the Berrys.

In these pages I have spoken almost indifferently of these sisters in the singular and the plural. And this is, in truth, a fair representation of their relation to one another. It was said that after Mary's unhappy engagement their friendship was lessened; but there is no sign of it in the biography. They appear on the scene sometimes single, sometimes double, owing to the sororal condition perhaps more than the elder and the abler would willingly have accepted. Agnes, it is clear, would have been nothing above an amiable, cheery, pretty, woman, but for Mary's superiority; yet it is undeniable that her liveliness was a most necessary compliment to Miss Berry's graver disposition, and that it was hard to say which was the greater gainer by the faculties of the other. During an illness, in which Mary was supposed to be seriously attacked, I was present when Mr. Rogers came to see her, not having visited the house for many years previous.

She received him with great kindness, but, after some strong expressions of sympathy, Agnes, bearing no longer what she, I think wrongly, believed to be a false and barren exhibition of feeling, burst out, ' You might have been, and you were not, anything to us when we were living, and you now come and insult us with your civilities when we are nigh dead.' This was a specimen of the more passionate, and, it may be, one-sided nature, which Agnes never concealed, and which time did not subdue.

Agnes died first, and Mary Berry went on for a short time bravely enduring life. But within the year the sisters lay together in the pleasant grave-yard of Petersham, close to the scenes which they had inspired with so many happy associations. To few it is given, as to these, to retain in extreme old age not only the clearness of the head but the brightness of the heart—to leave in those about them no sense of relief from the wayward second-childishness which so sadly rounds the life of man, but a pure regret that these almost patriarchal lives could not have lasted still longer.

The following lines, which appeared in the 'Times' the day after the funeral, embody in

verse the thoughts and feelings of which their life
was the expression :—

Two friends within one grave we place,
　　United in our tears,
Sisters, scarce parted for the space
　　Of more than eighty years;
And she, whose bier is borne to-day
　　The one the last to go,
Bears with her thoughts that force their way
　　Above the moment's woe :

Thoughts of the varied human life
　　Spread o'er that field of time,
The toil, the passion, and the strife,
　　The virtue and the crime :
Yet 'mid the long tumultuous scene,
　　The image on our mind
Of these dear women rests serene
　　In happy bounds confined.

Within one undisturbed abode
　　Their presence seems to dwell,
From which continual pleasures flowed,
　　And countless graces fell ;
Not unbecoming this our age
　　Of decorative forms,
Yet simple as the hermitage
　　Exposed to Nature's storms.

Our English grandeur on the shelf
　　Deposed its decant gloom :
And every pride unloosed itself
　　Within that modest room;
Where none were sad and few were dull,
　　And each one said his best,
And beauty was most beautiful
　　With vanity at rest.

Brightly the day's discourse rolled on,
    Still casting on the shore
Memorial pearls of times by-gone
    And worthies now no more.
And little tales of long ago,
    Took meaning from those lips,
Wise chroniclers of joy and woe,
    And eyes without eclipse.

No taunt or scoff obscured the wit
    That there rejoiced to reign ;
They never would have laughed at it
    If it had carried pain.
There needless scandal, e'en though true,
    Provoked no bitter smile,
And even men-of-fashion grew
    Benignant for awhile.

Not that there lacked the nervous scorn
    At every public wrong,
Not that a friend was left forlorn
    When victim of the strong ;
Free words expressing generous blood
    No nice punctilio weighed,
For deep an earnest womanhood
    Their reason underlaid.

As generations onward came,
    They loved from all to win
Revival of the sacred flame
    That glowed their hearts within ·
While others in time's greedy mesh
    The faded garlands flung,
Their hearts went out and gathered fresh
    Affections from the young.

Farewell, dear Ladies! in your loss
    We feel the past recede,

The gap, our hands could almost cross,
　Is now a gulf indeed.
Ye, and the days in which your claims
　And charms were early known,
Lose substance, and ye stand as names
　That Hist'ry makes it own.

Farewell! the pleasant social page
　Is read ; but ye remain
Examples of ennobled age,
　Long life without a stain ;
A lesson to be scorned by none,
　Least by the wise and brave,
Delightful as the winter sun
　That gilds this open grave.

HARRIET LADY ASHBURTON.

the and the work own short
the of any rec
duce
c

the ant
to give en
insig acts and p ssip connected
th their in life the att attitudes of
st claimants to distinction
ke Mrs. Elizabeth ntag
ves have lapped ov
and who accumulate by
m tude of small a soci

ASHBURTON.

VI.

HARRIET LADY ASHBURTON.

WHEN the successful Orator, Actor, Journalist, and Pamphleteer, must be content, in the main, with the fame and the work of their own short day, from the inability of any record or biography to reproduce their impression on mankind, how are the social celebrities of any time to live even here beyond the shifting-scene, in which they have played their part? And yet the world (more grateful perhaps for having been pleased than for having been instructed) is not unwilling to invest them with a personal interest and sympathy that the important figures of the part rarely obtain, and to give even to insignificant facts and pointless gossip connected with their place in life the airs and attitudes of ' History.' The fairest claimants to this distinction are, no doubt, women like Mrs. Elizabeth Montague or Miss Berry, whose lives have lapped over generations of mankind, and who accumulate by the mere lapse of time a multitude of small associations with

10

intellectual and political celebrities around their names. But I am here desirous to continue the recollection of a lady, whose sphere of action was limited, both in extent and in duration ; and whose peculiar characteristics rather impeded than promoted her position in an order of society where any strong individuality is both rare and unwelcome.

It is hard to conjecture what would have been the destiny of so complex a character in the ordinary struggle for existence : whether its nobler qualities would have made their way above the wilfulness and self-assertion that isolated and encumbered it ? whether the wonderful humour that relieved by its insight, and elevated by its imagination, the natural rudeness of her temperament and despotism of her disposition, might not have degenerated into cynicism and hatred ? Enough that here for once the accidents of birth and wealth resulted in giving liberty of thought and action to an ingenuous spirit, and at the same time placed it under the controul, not of manners alone, but of the sense of high state and large responsibility. She was an instance in which aristocracy gave of its best and showed at its best ; although she may have owed little to the qualities she inherited from an irascible race, and to an unaffectionate education. She often alluded to the hard repression of her childhood, and its effects. 'I was constantly punished for my impertinence, and you see the result. I think I have made up for it since.'

For many years before the husband of Lady Harriet Baring succeeded to his father's title and estates, Bath House and The Grange had been centres of a most agreeable and diversified society. The first Lord Ashburton combined great knowledge, experience, and discrimination, with a rare benignity of character and simplicity of manner. During his long career in the House of Commons the general moderation and breadth of his opinions had had the usual result of failing to command an Assembly that prefers any resolute error to judicious ambiguity; but, at the same time, these qualities had secured to him the personal esteem of the leading men of both parties. Thus his house was long a neutral ground for political intercourse, the prevalent tone being Tory, but of that aspect of Toryism which was fast lapsing into the Conservative Liberalism of Sir Robert Peel and Lord Aberdeen. The vast monetary negotiations in which Lord Ashburton had been engaged in various parts of the world—from the time when, almost as a boy, he transacted the sale of Louisiana to the United

States, to the conclusion of the long Continental
War, brought to his table every remarkable foreign
personage who visited this country, and with the
most distinguished of whom—King Leopold, for
instance—he had close personal relations. The
House of Baring, by marriage and community of
interests, was as much American as British, and
offered its hospitality to every eminent citizen of
the United States. The cordial reception of artists
was the natural concomitant of the taste and
wealth that illuminated the walls with the rarest
and most delightful examples of ancient and
modern Art, now, with few exceptions, lost to his
family and the world for ever, by one of those
lamentable accidents which no individual care, and
no mechanical appliance, seem adequate to prevent or to remedy. Nor was the literary element
wanting, though it generally found access through
some channel of political or personal intimacy. In
such company—in which a young woman even of
high social or intellectual claims might well have
passed unobserved—Lady Harriet at once took a
high and independent position, while towards her
husband's family and connections she assumed a
demeanour of superiority that at the time gave just
offence, and which later efforts and regrets never

wholly obliterated.   I am inclined to attribute this
defect of conduct rather to a wilful repugnance
towards any associations that seemed fixed upon
her by circumstances or obligation, and not of her
own free choice—a feeling which manifested itself
just as decidedly towards her own relatives—rather
than to any pride of birth, or even haughtiness of
disposition.   I remember her saying, 'The worst
of being very ill is that one is left to the care of
one's relations, and one has no remedy at law,
whatever they may be.'   On the other hand, we
may well recollect the scathing irony with which
she treated excessive genealogical pretensions, especially among her own connections ; while she
never concealed her sense of the peculiar national
importance and commercial dignity of the 'Barings.'
'They are everywhere,' she said, 'they get everything.   The only check upon them is that they are
all members of the Church of England ; otherwise
there is no saying what they would do.'

It was the natural effect of this independence of
any domestic circle, or even of any society of
which she was not herself the centre and the chief,
which induced Lady Harriet Baring to collect
around her a small body of friends, of which her
own singular talent was the inspiring spirit.   Thus

when, in the course of events, she became the head of the family, she was at once able, not only to sustain the social repute of the former generation, but to stamp it with a special distinction. I do not know how I can better describe this faculty than as the fullest and freest exercise of an intellectual gaiety, that presented the most agreeable and amusing pictures in few and varied words; making high comedy out of daily life, and relieving sound sense and serious observation with imaginative contrasts and delicate surprises. It is unnecessary to say that this power, combined with such a temperament as I have described, was eminently dangerous, and could not but occasionally descend into burlesque and caricature; and in the personal talk with which English society abounds, it could not keep altogether clear of satirical injustice. But to those who had the opportunity of watching its play, and tracing its motives, there was an entire absence of that ill-nature which makes ridicule easy; and even when apparently cruel, it was rather the outburst of a judicial severity than of a wanton unkindness. In the conversational combats thus provoked, the woman no doubt frequently took the woman's advantage, and attacked where no defence was decorously possible; but the impulse was always to measure herself with the strong—not to triumph over the weak.

But while persons cognisant of the art, and appreciative of her rapidity of movement and dexterity of fence, were fully sympathetic with Princess Lieven's judgment, '*Qu'il vaudrait bien s'abonner pour entendre causer cette femme,*' there were many estimable people to whom the electric transition from grave to gay was thoroughly distasteful ; and there were others who, distanced in the race of thought and expression, went away with a sense of humiliation or little inclination to return. Many who would not have cared for a quiet defeat, shrank from the merriment of her victory. I remember one of them saying : ' I do not mind being knocked down, but I can't stand being danced upon afterwards.' It was in truth a joyous sincerity that no conventionalities, high or low, could restrain—a festive nature flowering through the artificial soil of elevated life.

There could be no better guarantee of these qualities than the constant friendship that existed between Lady Ashburton and Mr. Carlyle—on her part one of filial respect and duteous admiration. The frequent presence of the great moralist of itself gave to the life of Bath House and The Grange a

reality that made the most ordinary worldly com-
ponent parts of it more human and worthy than
elsewhere.   The very contact of a conversation
which was always bright, and never frivolous,
brought out the best elements of individual
character, reconciled formal politicians with free
men of letters and men of pleasure with those
that bear the burden of the day.   'Ask me to
meet your printers,' was the often-quoted speech
of a lady of fashion.   Of course there are barriers in
our social life which no individual will or power can
throw down.   You cannot bring into close sympathetic communion the operative poor and the in-
operative rich any more in intellectual than in
physical relations, but all that was possible was
here done.   Patronage was neither given nor taken:
if the person suited the society, and showed by his
contribution or his enjoyment that he did so, he
might be quite sure of its continuance; otherwise
he left it, without much notice taken on one side
or the other.   That this was not always so, an
amusing passage between Mr. Thackeray and Lady
Ashburton illustrates.   Having been most kindly
received, he took umbrage at some hard rallying,
perhaps rather of others than of himself, and not
only declined her invitations, but spoke of her with

discourtesy and personal dislike. After some months, when the angry feeling on his part had had time to die out, he received from her a card of invitation to dinner. He returned it, with an admirable drawing on the back, representing himself kneeling at her feet with his hair all aflame from the hot coals she was energetically pouring on his head out of an ornamental brazier. This act of contrition was followed by a complete reconciliation, and much friendship on her part towards him and his family.

But although such men were admitted to her intimacy, and all men-of-letters or promising aspirants were welcomed to her larger assemblies, the chief intimates of the house were men of public life, either in Parliament or the Press, with no exclusion of party, but with an inclination towards the politics which her husband supported. As Mr. Bingham Baring he had formed part of the administration of Sir Robert Peel in 1835, and had all the mind and thought of a statesman, but was deficient in those aptitudes which enable a man to make the most of his talents, and present them with effect to others. He had that shyness which often belongs to Englishmen of great capacity and knowledge, and to which those faculties themselves,

10*

in a certain degree, contribute.   By the very power
of appreciation of the breadth and gravity of affairs,
by the very insight into the merits of men and things,
by their very sense of the moral and intellectual
defects of those to whom the world accords favour
and honour, such men give an impression of
mental weakness, and even of moral inferiority;
whereas they have within them all the real elements
of governing force, and on a right occasion will
frequently exhibit them.   When such qualities are
combined, as they were in Lord Ashburton, with
the noblest and purest purpose, with an entirely
unselfish and truthful disposition, and with a
determination to fulfil every duty of his station,
from the lowest to the highest, they may excite
in them that know and love them best a sense of
the deep injustice done to them by public opinion,
and an ardent desire to remedy it.   Thus Lady
Ashburton lost no opportunity to stimulate her
husband's ambition, and was anxious above all
things to make her own great social position
subservient to his public fortunes; and yet, by one
of the mischances which attend the combinations of
human character, her very eminence damaged his
consideration, and his affection and admiration for
her were the instruments of his comparative insig-

nificance. There was something offensive to the sense of English independence in the constant enjoyment he took in the display of her genius and effervescence of her gaiety. It was in truth a concurrence of lover-like delight and intellectual wonder, and those who saw in it a slavish submission were unconscious of the quiet authority he assumed in all the serious concerns of life, and the gradual moulding of the violent and angular parts of her nature, under the correction of his moral elevation and the experience of his gentle wisdom. Nor indeed was there any want of his influence even in the field of ordinary society. He had an unquenchable thirst for information, and brought about him every special capacity and all sound learning. I never knew anyone with a keener sense of imposture or a shrewder detection of superficial knowledge. In this his intellect was but the reflection of his moral self, which had so entire an abhorrence of falsehood that I have often thought it was saved from a pedantry of veracity by the humoristic atmosphere with which it was surrounded. But though thus in a certain degree reconciled to the common transactions of political and social life, yet it always maintained a certain isolation which prevented him from becoming the ready comrade of ordinary practical men, or the handy colleague of any Government.

I have no intention of painting a group of The Grange, but there was one member of this goodly company so constant and so conspicuous, so united to it by ties of intellectual sympathy, that I may well profit by the introduction of his name to satisfy my own feelings of gratitude and affection. Mr. Bingham Baring had made the acquaintance of Mr. Charles Buller in Madeira, where he had accompanied a dying brother. The opportunities which so often bring Englishmen together in close relations in a foreign country, resulted in an earnest friendship between the young men, which was afterwards cemented by an introduction to Mr. Buller's family, and its remarkable society, that included Mr. (now Sir) Henry Taylor, Mr. John Sterling, and Mr. Thomas Carlyle. Lady Harriet fully shared her husband's esteem for Mr. Buller and enjoyment of his social qualities. Now that death had swept off with such a strange rapidity the public men who began their career about the time of the first Reform Bill, and who for the most part became the pupils and followers of Sir Robert Peel, it must not be forgotten that there sat on the opposite bench one for whom the House of Commons

CHARLES BULLER.

... ... practical men, or the handy
... ... Government.

... intention of painting a group of Th...
... ... was one member of this goodly
... ... so conspicuous, so
united ... by ties of intellectual sympathy, th...
I may well profit by the introduction of his
name to satisfy my own feelings of gratitude
... Bingham Baring had made the
... Charles Buller in Madeira,
... ... a dying brother. The
opp... ... so often bring. Englishmen
together in close relations in a foreign country,
resulted in an earnest friendship between the young
men, which was afterwards cemented by an introduction to Mr. Buller's family, and its remarkable
circle, which included Mr. (now Sir) Henry Taylor,
... ... and Mr. Thomas Carlyle. Lady
... her husband's esteem for Mr.
... ... of his social qualities. Now
... ... off with such a strange rapidity
... ... who began their career about the time
... ... Reform Bill, and who for the most part
became the pupils and followers of Sir Robert Peel,
it must not be forgotten that there sat on the opposite bench one for whom the House of Commons

CHARLES BULLER.

predicted as brilliant a success as for any member of the other party. Mr. Buller had been fortunate in identifying himself with a question now trite enough, but then pregnant with interest to masses of men and the destinies of the world. To replace the quarrelsome relations between the British Colonies and the Home Government (then personified in Sir James Stephen, who bore the *sobriquet* of 'Mother-country') by a system which would at once de-velope the faculties of the Anglo-Saxon race, and relieve England from its weight of pauperism by systematic emigration, was a project of high practical purpose and beneficial hope. With him, as comrades in the cause, were the present Lord Grey and the late Sir William Molesworth, who, taken away in the prime of life, but not without having attained high political office, holds his place among the statesmen of his country. Mr. Buller had the important advantage of having been employed in the pacification of Canada, as Secretary to Lord Durham, and had had the credit of drawing up the Report, which was generally approved, without sharing the discomfiture that fell on some of the official conductors of the negotiation. The Colonial policy thus initiated has since run its full course, and though not attended with all the magnificent effects then anticipated, and at the present moment rather veering in its direction, has nevertheless left its mark on the history of the world, and offers in its integrity the only possible solution of the problem of the future migrations of the British race.

My own relations with Charles Buller dated from Cambridge; and when I entered the House of Commons, he had won the ear of the House not only on his special question, but on all the great agitations of the day. During many years I found in him an affectionate friend and judicious counsellor, not less when we belonged to different parties than when the conversion of Sir Robert Peel to the policy of Free Trade in corn broke up the Government, and sent his followers to make new combinations, as best suited the opinions they had acquired or maintained.

As an episode in our intimacy, I am glad to remember a *jeu d'esprit* which we concocted on the occasion of the Queen's first Fancy Ball, where the chief characters of the court and times of King Edward the Third were represented. This was a supposed debate in the French Chamber of Deputies on the preceding day, reported ' by express ' in the ' Morning Chronicle : ' originating in an interpellation of M. Berryer, to the effect—' Whether the French Ambassador in England had been invited to the *bal masqué* which is to be given by the haughty descendant of the Plantagenets for the purpose of awakening the long-buried griefs of France in the disasters of Cressy and Poictiers and the loss of Calais.' This speech, by Buller, is an excellent imitation of the great orator's manner, though I remember protesting against the grotesqueness of the demand 'Whether M. de St. Aulaire was going with his *attachés*, with bare feet and halters round their necks, representing the unfortunate Burgesses?' It concluded with the declamation—'It is on the banks of the Rhine that the cannon of France ought to accompany the dancers of St. James's. It is by taking the Ballearic Isles that we should efface the recollections of Agincourt.' I followed in the name of M. de Lamartine, reproving the speaker with talking of the 'vilification of France,' and saying France could well afford to leave to each people its own historical traditions.—' Ah! let them have their splendid *guinguette*—that people at once so grave and frivolous. Let them dance as they please, as long as the great mind of France calmly and nobly traverses the world.' Lamartine was answered by M. de Tocqueville (also mine) finding fault with the

ball chiefly as a repudiation of the democratic idea,
and a mournful reaction against the spirit of the
times; saying, with a sad and grave impartiality,
—'We too have erred—we too have danced and
costumed—the heirs of the throne of July have
sanctioned this frivolity, but there was no quadrille
of the Heroes of Fontenoy!' M. Guizot (Buller)
closed the discussion by stating that Lord Aberdeen had given the most satisfactory explanations
—that the Queen of England desired to educate
her people by a series of archæological enter-
tainments; but that, in deference to the susceptibilities of France, M. de St. Aulaire would represent
the Virgin of Domremy—he would go as 'Joan of
Arc.' It seems incredible that what we meant for a
political squib should have turned out a successful
hoax. It was discussed with gravity in the clubs;
and, at the ball itself, Sir Robert Peel told me,
with great satisfaction, that Sir James Graham had
rushed into his private rooms in Whitehall Gardens
with the paper in his hand, exclaiming, 'There is
the devil to pay in France about this foolish ball.'
But the Press was the most deluded victim: the
'Irish Pilot' remarked that 'the fact of so slight an
occasion having given rise to so grave a discussion
is the strongest evidence of the state of feeling in

France towards this country.' The 'Dumfries Courier' commented at much length on this 'as one of the most erratic and ridiculous scenes that ever lowered the dignity of a deliberative assembly.' The 'Sémaphore de Marseilles' translated the article into French as a faithful report, and the 'Commerce' indignantly protested against the taste for a masquerade going so far as 'to allow the panoply of a woman so cruelly sacrificed to British pride to be worn on such an occasion.' Others formally denied that the genuine armour had ever been sent from Paris. It is only fair to remark that at the time France had been violently excited by Lord Palmerston's Syrian policy, and that England was believed capable of anything that might degrade or injure her.

A short time afterwards Buller added to our political *Facetiæ* a Latin letter, addressed by the Vice-Chancellor of Oxford to the members of the Senate, urging them to vote for the abrogation of the Statute passed in 1836 against Dr. Hampden, and which is proudly announced as 'not written in the language of the Papal schism.' An extract is worth preserving as a specimen of its sound humour, and in its exposition of the clerical politics of the time reminding the historical reader of the 'Epistolæ

Obscurorum Virorum,' and the ecclesiastics of their day. Even those were not without believers in their authenticity! One writer (1515) expresses his wonder ' why such great men should be called '' obscure." '

' Radicales sunt penitus eversi : Peelus est in potentiâ. Peelus autem in potentiâ est res totaliter differens Peelo in oppositione. Si tutò possemus subvertere illum, non singulum momentum in officio maneret, quia nobis videtur facere omnia ea quibus alii tantum loquebantur de. Videte autem, fratres carissimi ! in quâ lamentabili positione ponuntur Ecclesia, amicique Ecclesiæ ! *Si subvertimus Peelum, mortuæ certitudini habebimus Johannulum.* Hæc est res non singulo momento contemplanda. Necesse est igitur ut faciamus quodcunque vult Peelus. Peelus vult pretendere esse liberalis ; necesse igitur est ut nos etiam liberales esse pretenderemus. Et ut condemnatio Doctoris Hampden opus suum omnino peregit, sine ullo damno possumus liberalem cursum incipere revocando illam.'

These reminiscences of Charles Buller's special intellectual characteristic will suggest the consideration whether, though accompanied as it was with strong common sense and a clear intuition into political theories and conditions, it would not have seriously affected and probably have endangered his political career had he lived to pursue it to its legitimate end. Experience in the House of Commons teaches that while wit is an invaluable element in parliamentary discussion, humour is worthless or detrimental. Images and arguments that in the mind of the humoristic speaker in no way derogate from the dignity of his subject, seem irrevelant or degrading to those who are without the apprehensive faculty. This effect probably applies to any large and mixed audience, where the majority must always be deficient in the finer perceptions. It is, therefore, doubtful whether Charles Buller could have so restrained his grotesque fancy as to have avoided an impression of flippancy and insincerity, and conformed himself to the traditions of official demeanour which the English people approve in their governors.

He died very unexpectedly after a slight operation, showing great weakness of natural constitution. A fortnight before he had been the life of a large party at The Grange, where his place was never filled again. An accident in infancy had seriously damaged his good looks, but certainly did not authorise the impression of cynicism and satiric obliquity which some persons, strangers to

his most amiable disposition, professed to find in
his countenance. Those indeed who knew him
well could see a certain tender and even pathetic
grace beneath the deformity, which Mr. Weekes
has rendered with great skill in the bust in Westminster Abbey. This work of art is the more admirable, as the sculptor had to compose it out of
posthumous materials.   I remember when I went,
by Lord and Lady Ashburton's desire, to Dr. Buck-
land, then Dean of Westminster, to take his pleasure as to the erection of the monument, he not
only received the request with hearty concurrence,
but himself selected the position—close to that of
Horner ; remarking that ' they would stand well
together from the similarity of their early distinction and premature deaths.'   I give the Epitaph I
had the privilege to compose as the best summary
of my estimate of his moral and intellectual attributes.

HERE, AMIDST THE MEMORIALS OF MATURER GREATNESS,
THIS TRIBUTE OF PRIVATE AFFECTION AND PUBLIC HONOUR
RECORDS THE TALENTS, VIRTUES, AND EARLY DEATH OF
THE RIGHT HONOURABLE CHARLES BULLER :
WHO, AS AN INDEPENDENT MEMBER OF PARLIAMENT,
AND IN THE DISCHARGE OF IMPORTANT OFFICES OF STATE,
UNITED THE DEEPEST HUMAN SYMPATHIES
WITH WIDE AND PHILOSOPHIC VIEWS OF GOVERNMENT
AND MANKIND,

AND PURSUED THE NOBLEST POLITICAL AND SOCIAL OBJECTS,
ABOVE PARTY SPIRIT AND WITHOUT AN ENEMY.
HIS CHARACTER WAS DISTINGUISHED BY SINCERITY AND RESO-
LUTION,
HIS MIND BY VIVACITY AND CLEARNESS OF COMPREHENSION ;
WHILE THE VIGOUR OF EXPRESSION AND SINGULAR WIT,
THAT MADE HIM EMINENT IN DEBATE AND DELIGHTFUL IN
SOCIETY,
WERE TEMPERED BY A MOST GENTLE AND GENEROUS DISPO-
SITION,
EARNEST IN FRIENDSHIP AND DELIGHTFUL TO ALL.
THE BRITISH COLONIES WILL NOT FORGET THE STATESMAN
WHO SO WELL APPRECIATED THEIR DESIRES AND THEIR
DESTINIES,
AND HIS COUNTRY, RECALLING WHAT HE WAS, DEPLORES
THE VANISHED HOPE OF ALL HE MIGHT HAVE BECOME.
HE WAS BORN AUGUST 6, 1806. HE DIED NOVEMBER 29, 1848.

The manner of life at The Grange did not differ from that of our best country-houses. The comforts and appliances incidental to the condition were there without notice or apparent care : and there was that highest luxury which the wealthiest so rarely enjoy—the ease of riches. Lady Ashburton met her guests at breakfast, but was recommended by her medical advisers to dine early in her own room. This arrangement enabled her to initiate and direct the conversation at dinner with no other distraction, and to combine the fullest exercise of her own faculty with the skilful observation and exhibition of the powers of all around the

table. There was no avoidance of special or professional topics ; and the false delicacy which so
often induces modern talk to shun the very chan-
nels into which it can run the most naturally and
the fullest, would have no place, where every man
felt that he would be respected and admired for
what he really was, and for what he knew
the best, and where all pretensions fell before
the liberty and equality of Humour. At the
same time there was a decided restraint, by no
means agreeable to those accustomed to the looser
treatment of delicate subjects permitted in many
refined circles, and who were annoyed at the cool
reception given even to brilliant talk on equivocal
matter.

It was with no disregard of her sex that Lady
Ashburton preferred the society of men. Having
lost her only child by a sad mischance, she shrank
from the sympathies of family life, and avoided topics that might suggest useless regrets. Nearly the
whole of her female companions were in the same
domestic position as herself, and yet to children
generally, and especially to those of her intimates,
she was kind and even affectionate. In young
women of personal attractions she took a deep
interest, and I know no better summary of the

place and circumstances than that of one who still adorns the world, who, I remember, in answer to some question as to her stay there, replied, ' I never count days at the Grange: I only know that it is morning when I come, and night when I go away.'

I will now place within this slight framework some reminiscences of Lady Ashburton's thoughts and expressions—faint but faithful echoes of living speech. They must not be regarded as considered apothegms, or even fixed opinions, but as the rapid and almost interjectional utterances of dialogue, replying, interrupting, anticipating, with a magnetic prescience, the coming words, checking and often crushing any rising contradiction. They will seem, I doubt not, in many points hardly reconcilable with the outline of character that I have drawn—almost ironical negatives of the very qualities I have ascribed to her—but yet they are thoroughly true in relation to her deeper self, and though paradoxes in part, they do not only shut the door one ommonplace, but let in some clearer and wider light.

(Of Herself):

How fortunate that I am not married to King Leopold! He said to his French wife, ' *Pas de propos légers.'* I suppose he meant ' No jokes.' Now I like nothing else—I should wish to be accountable for nothing I said, and to contradict myself every minute.

It is dreadful for me to have no domestic duties. I always envy the German women. I am a ' cuisinière incomprise.'

(In London)—You say it is a fine day, and wish me to go out. How can I go out ? Ordering one's carriage, and waiting for it, and getting into it : that is not ' going out.' If I were a shopkeeper's wife I would go out when and where and how I pleased.

If I am to go into London society, and sit for hours by Lord ——, all I say is, I shall be carried out.

I always feel a kind of average between myself and any other person I am talking with—between us two, I mean : so that when I am talking to Spedding—I am unutterably foolish—beyond permission.*

Can I do everything at once ? Am I Briareus ?

I like you to say the civil things, and then I can do the contrary.

* Lady Ashburton called her intimate friends by their surnames, when speaking of or to them, after the usual fashion of an older time.

What with the cold water in which I am plunged in the morning, and the cold water thrown upon me in the day, life in England is intolerable.

In one's youth one doubts whether one has a body, and when one gets old whether one has a soul; but the body asserts itself so much the stronger of the two.

I have not only never written a book, but I know nobody whose book I should like to have written.

I remember when a child telling everybody I was present at mamma's marriage. I was whipped for it, but I believed it all the same.

(Would it not be the death of you to live a year with —— ?). No; I should not die. I should kill.

When I passed by Bennett's church in the morning, all dressed in my diamonds and flowers, to be drawn by Swinton, the beadle in full costume bowed low to me, taking me for an altar-piece or something to be reverenced.

When I am with High-Church people, my opposition to them makes me feel no church at all— hardly bare walls with doors and windows.

I forget everything, except injuries.

(Of Morals and Men) :

I should like exactly to know the difference between money and morality.

11

I have no objection to the canvas of a man's mind being good if it is entirely hidden under the worsted and floss, and so on.

Public men in England are so fenced in by the cactus-hedge of petty conventionality which they call practical life, that everything good and humane is invisible to them. Add to this the absence of humour, and you see all their wretchedness. I have never known but two men above this—Buller and Peel.

Coming back to the society of Carlyle after the dons at Oxford is like returning from some conventional world to the human race.

A bore cannot be a good man : for the better a man is, the greater bore he will be, and the more hateful he will make goodness.

I am sure you will find nine persons out of ten, what at first you assumed them to be.

(To the remark that liars generally speak good-naturedly of others), Why, if you don't speak a word of truth, it is not so difficult to speak well of your neighbour.

—— has only two ideas, and they are his legs, and they are spindle-shanked.

('Don't speak so hard of —— ; he lives on your good graces.') That accounts for his being so thin.

(Of an Indian official) : What can you expect of a man who has been always waited on by Zemindars and lived with Zemindees ?

When —— speaks in public you have a different feeling from that of hearing most persons ; you wish he was doing it better.

(To Mr. Carlyle): How are you to-day ? 'Battling with Chaos !' 'In this house you might have said Cosmos.' (Again to Mr. Carlyle's denunciation,) 'Send him to Chaos.' 'You can't.'—'Why ?' 'It's full.'

—— has nothing truly human about him ; he cannot even yawn like a man.

(Of Marriage and Friendship) :

When one sees what marriage generally is, I quite wonder that women do not give up the profession.

You seem to think that married people always want events to talk about: I wonder what news Adam used to bring to Eve of an afternoon.

Your notion of a wife is evidently a Strasbourg goose whom you will always find by the fireside when you come home from amusing yourself.

Of course there will be slavery in the world as long as there is a black and a white—a man and a woman.

I am strongly in favour of Polygamy. I should

like to go out, and the other wife to stay at home and take care of things, and hear all I had to tell her when I came back.

—— looks all a woman wants—strength and cruelty.

The most dreadful thing against women is the character of the men that praise them.

However bad —— may be, I will not give him up. ' J'ai mes *devoirs.*'

I like men to be men; you cannot get round them without.

Friendship has no doubt great advantages; you know a man so much better and can laugh at him so much more.

If I were to begin life again, I would go on the turf, merely to get friends : they seem to me the only people who really hold close together. I don't know why : it may be that each man knows something that might hang the other; but the effect is delightful and most peculiar.

I never want friends if I have sun—or at most one who does not speak.

Now that you have picked my dearest friend to the bone, let me say of him . . .

(Of Society and Conversation) :

To have a really agreeable house, you must be

divorced; you would then have the pleasantest men, and no women but those who are really affectionate and interested about you, and who are kept in continual good-humour by the consciousness of a benevolent patronage. I often think of divorcing myself from B. B. and marrying him again.

My 'printers,' as they call them, have become a sort of Order of the Garter. I dare not talk to these knights as I could do to fine ladies and gentlemen.

She never speaks to any one, which is of course a great advantage to any one.

He mentioned that 'his son was deaf,' and we could do no more than say that we preferred the deaf people to all others, except the dumb.

There is no rebound about'her: it is like talking into a soft surface.

Is —— the man who has padded the walls of his bedroom to be ready when he goes mad?

Talking to —— is like playing long whist.

What is the most melancholy song you can sing?

How high-bred that rhymed conversation of the French classic comedy sounds! I could fancy —— always talking in that way.

There is as much fun in —— as can live in all that gold and lace and powder.

English society is destroyed by domestic life out of place. You meet eight people at dinner—four couples, each of whom sees as much as they wish of one another elsewhere, and each member of which is embarrassed and afraid in the other's presence.

The imperfect health against which Lady Ashburton had long struggled with so much magnanimity resulted in a serious illness at Nice in 1857, and she died with resignation and composure at Paris, on her way to England. She was buried in the quiet churchyard, near to the home her presence had gladdened and elevated. The funeral service was read by the present Archbishop of Dublin, for many years incumbent of the family living of Itchinstoke, and worthy friend of the house. Around the vault stood an assembly of men foremost in the political and literary history of their time, who felt that there ended for all of them much of the charm of English society, and for many the enjoyment of a noble friendship. In his bitter sorrow, Lord Ashburton did not forget, to use his own words, ' the singular felicity that had been accorded to him in more than thirty years of unclouded happiness in the companionship of this gifted woman.'

VII.

THE REV. SYDNEY SMITH.

WHEN Lady Holland, the wife of the eminent physician and natural philosopher, undertook the biography of her father, she applied to me and others for any reminiscences we might happen to have retained of his familiar life and conversation. The greater part of the material I supplied to her is incorporated in her admirable and accessible volumes, and I am unwilling to repeat it here. But something remains which I do not think has been given to the public, and there are aspects of the character of my old friend and social companion which have not been made as prominent as they deserve.

As a Yorkshireman I had heard much of the inspiring effects of his wit and gaiety in provincial life, and his residences among the breezy wolds of the East Riding are still pointed out with respectful interest. In that country, which still retains its pastoral character, and where the simple

11*

habits of a sparse and scattered population offer a
striking contrast to the fume and tumult of their
Western neighbours, there had been erected during
the last and former centuries, by a strange accident
of aristocratic possession, and at a cost which the
difficulties of transport and the facility of labour
at the time of their construction must have rendered enormous, some of the noblest and most
decorated of English mansions. The inhabitants
of these isolated palaces, of which Castle Howard
is the most notable, welcomed with delight the
unexpected vicinage of a mighty Edinburgh Re-
viewer in the disguise of a village parson, and
competed for his society with the not distant city
of York, over the church of which Archbishop
Harcourt, the last of the Cardinal Prelates of our
Establishment, so long presided.

This intercourse not only relieved what would
have been a sad change from the genial hospital-
ities and frequent festivities of his former city
life, but increased that familiar and friendly
association with the representatives of a higher
station in society which alone made it agreeable,
or even tolerable, to his independent nature. He
demanded equality, at least, in every company he
entered, and generally got something more.

I have heard that it took some time for his professional brethren to accommodate themselves to what would have been indeed a startling apparition in their retired and monotonous existence, but that his active interest in parochial matters, however insignificant, his entire simplicity of demeanour, his cheerful endurance and ingenious remedies in all the little discomforts of his position, quite won their hearts, and that he became as popular with them as ever he was among his cognate wits and intellectual fellows. He willingly assisted his neighbours in their clerical duties, and an anecdote of one of these occasions is still current in the district, for the authenticity of which I will not vouch, but which seems to me good enough to be true. He dined with the incumbent on the preceding Saturday, and the evening passed in great hilarity, the squire, by name Kershaw, being conspicuous for his loud enjoyment of the stranger's jokes. ' I am very glad that I have amused you,' said Mr. Sydney Smith at parting, ' but you must not laugh at my sermon to-morrow.' ' I should hope I know the difference between being here or at church,' remarked the gentleman with some sharpness. ' I am not so sure of that,' replied the visitor; ' I'll bet you a guinea on it,' said the squire. ' Take you,' replied the divine. The preacher ascended the steps of the pulpit apparently suffering from a severe cold, with his handkerchief to his face, and at once *sneezed* out the name 'Ker-shaw' several times in various intonations. This ingenious assumption of the readiness with which a man would recognise his own name in sounds imperceptible to the ears of others, proved accurate. The poor gentleman burst into a guffaw, to the scandal of the congregation ; and the minister, after looking at him with stern reproach, proceeded with his discourse and won the bet.

Though in appearance less brilliant and important, I suspect that this must have been the happiest period of Mr. Sydney Smith's career. He had full health, talents employed, domestic comforts, great hopes of eminence in his profession, and abundant amusement without the inevitable frivolities that wait on large companies of men, or the moral and intellectual condescensions which great popularity in the social, as well as in the political, world demands.

The luxurious Somersetshire rectory to which he was soon transferred had many superior attractions to his rough Yorkshire home, but he never ceased to regret the fresh atmosphere and shrewd energy of the North. 'What with the long torpor of the cider, and the heated air of the west,' he said, ' they all become boozy, the squires grow blind, the labourers come drunk to work, and the maids pin their mistresses' gowns awry.' In his own phrase he 'eviscerated' the house and made it most commodious, and every wall glistened with books. But the great merit of Combe Florey was that, as he said, ' It bound up so well with London ; ' and when, on Lord Grey's accession to power, he was appointed to a Canonry of St. Paul's, he was able to oscillate agreeably between the two functions and to get the most out of Town and Country. It was a great delight to him to induce his London friends to visit him, and Lady Holland's work abounds with his devices and mystifications for their diversion. 'When Poodle Byng comes here,' he said, ' all the hedge-rows smell like Piccadilly ; ' * but he could not always hope for this result. The first time he invited me was in these terms :

' If you have really any intention of paying me a Visit, I must describe the " locale." We live six miles from Taunton on the Minehead road. You

---

* The Hon. Frederick Byng, a well-known Londoner whose long social life has lately closed—Page of Honour at the marriage of one Prince of Wales in 1796, and Gentleman Usher at the marriage of another in 1863,—'*nommé,*' according to a French commentator on London society, ' *à cause de sa fidélité, Poodle.*'

must give me good notice, and await my answer, for we are often full and often sick. It is but fair to add that nothing can be more melancholy and stupid than Combe Florey—that we have no other neighbours than the Parsonism of the county, and that in the country I hybernate and lick my paws. Having stated these distressing truths, and assuring you that (as you like to lay out your life to the best advantage) it is not worth your while to come, I have only to add that we shall be very glad to see you.'

There was, as might be expected, much exaggeration in these melancholy prognostics, and I do not know that he was ever more interesting than when seen in the common round of small and familiar occupations which he invested with his own jocularity. The appropriate nicknames, the new significance given to local anecdote or personal peculiarity, the singular mixture of grin and reverence with which he was greeted by his rustic friends, and the serious converse to which the enforced leisure was favourable, made a visit to Combe Florey not only a pleasant but useful incident in life.

But his love of London it was impossible to overrate. The old Marquis who never approached the town without the ejaculation 'Those blessed lamps!' was far outstripped by his eloquent fancy. I remember his vision of an immense Square with the trees flowering with flambeaux, with gas for grass, and every window illuminated by countless chandeliers, and voices reiterating for ever and for ever, 'Mr. Sydney Smith coming up stairs!' The parallelogram between Hyde Park and Regent Street, Oxford Street and Piccadilly, within which he dwelt, contained, in his belief, more wisdom, wit, and wealth than all the rest of the inhabited globe. It was to him a magazine and repository of what was deepest and most real in human life. 'If a messenger from heaven,' he used to say, 'were on a sudden to annihilate the love of power, the love of wealth, the love of esteem, in the hearts of men, the streets of London would be as empty and silent at noon as they are now in the middle of the night.' His nature demanded for its satisfaction the fresh interests of every hour; he defined the country—'a place with only one post a day.' The little expectations and trivial disappointments, the notes and the responses, the news and the contradictions, the gossip and the refutation, were to him sources of infinite amusement; and the immense social popularity which made his presence at a dinner-table a household event, was satisfactory to his pleasure-loving and pleasure-giving temperament, even if it sometimes annoyed him in its indiscriminating exigency. The very diversity and, it may be, the frequent inferiority of the company in which he found himself was not distasteful to him, for while his cheerfulness made his own portion of the entertainment its own satisfaction, he had acquired, when I knew him, the habit of direction and mastery in almost every society where he found himself.   He would allow, what indeed he could not prevent, the brilliant monologue of Mr. Macaulay, and was content to avenge himself with the pleasantry, 'That he not only overflowed with learning, but stood in the slop.'   He yielded to the philosophy and erudition of such men as Dean Milman, and Mr. Grote, with an occasional deprecatory comment, but he admitted no competition or encounter in his own field. On this point he was strangely unjust.   When some enterprising entertainer brought him and Mr. Theodore Hook together, the failure was complete; Mr. Sydney Smith could see nothing but buffoonery in the gay, dramatic, faculty and wonderful extempore invention of the novelist, just as he either could, or would not, see any merit in those masterpieces of comic verse, the works of one of his own fellow-administrators of the cathedral of St. Paul's, the ' Ingoldsby Legends.'

Not that, in the common phrase, he monopolised the conversation ; it rather monopolised him, as was expressed by the young lady, who responded by a fit of laughter to his grace after dinner, exclaiming : ' You are always so amusing.'

There was, in truth, little inclination to talk in his presence, except for the purpose of directing him to topics on which he would be likely to be most salient ; and he willingly followed the lead, instead of insisting on his own line of thought, regardless whether the subject was of interest to his audience or not—a defect which no brilliancy of speech or power of argument can remedy, and which rendered all the acuteness and fluency of Archbishop Whately comparatively unattractive. Mr. Sydney Smith, on the contrary, was inspired by the sympathy of his hearers, and even interruptions, which showed an intelligent appreciation, were not disagreeable to him. The strongest phrase of approbation of the talent in others I ever heard from him was applied to a young man starting in London life : ' He will do ; he knows how to trump, but it will take him five years to play his own game.'

Those who happened to meet him continuously

would observe the growth of any subject that struck
his fancy; it would begin with some ludicrous observation, next rise into a picture, and accumulate
incidents by the very telling, till it rose into a full
imaginative anecdote.   For example, when certain
members of the Athenæum entertained M. Guizot,
in his double rank of French Ambassador and man
of letters, the story began with his reception by Mr.
Murray and Mr. Longman with white staves, then
his passing through Messrs. Rees, Orme and
Brown and so on, every day adding some fresh material of comic association till it culminated in the
French cook bursting into tears : *Mon pauvre
maître, je ne le reverrai plus!*

He has written depreciatingly of all playing
upon words, but his rapid apprehension could not
altogether exclude a kind of wit which in its best
forms takes fast hold of the memory, besides the
momentary amusement it excites.   His objection
to the superiority of a City feast: ' I cannot
wholly value a dinner by the test you do ; '—
his proposal to settle the question of the wood-
pavement round St. Paul's : ' Let the Canons once
lay their heads together, and the thing will be
done ; '—his pretty compliment to his friends,
Mrs. Tighe and Mrs. Cuffe : ' Ah ! there you are :

the cuff that every one would wear, the tie that no one would loose'—may be cited as perfect in their way. His salutation to a friend who had grown stouter, 'I did not half see you when you were in town last year,' is perhaps rather a play on thoughts than on words.

The irrepressible humour sometimes forced its way in a singular manner through serious observations. He was speaking of the accusations of nepotism brought against a statesman to whom he was much attached, and which he thought supremely unjust: 'Such a disposition of patronage was one of the legitimate inducements to a man of high rank and large fortune to abandon the comforts of private life for the turmoils and disappointments of a political career. Nor did the country suffer by it; on the contrary, a man was much more likely to be able to judge of the real competence of his relatives whom he knew well for any office than he could from second-hand or documentary information;—indeed, he felt this so strongly that, if by any inconceivable freak of fortune he himself were placed in the position, he should think himself not only authorised, but compelled, to give a competent post to every man of his own name in the country. Again, in the course of an argument on the sub-

ject of the interference of this country in foreign
wars, and the necessity of keeping up our national
prestige on the Continent, after some sound reason-
ing he concluded : ' I have spent enough and fought
enough for other nations.   I must think a little of
myself—I want to sit under my own bramble and
sloe-tree with my own great-coat and umbrella.
No war for me short of Piccadilly ; there, indeed,
in front of Grange's shop, I will meet Luttrell, and
Rogers, and Wilmot and other knights ; I will combat to the death for Fortnum and Mason's next door,
and fall in defence of the sauces of my country.'

While his main delight was in intellectual intercourse, and, during his more active life, in intellectual exertion, he could hardly be called a student
of literature.   He thought it no more necessary
for a man to remember the different books that had
made him wise than the different dinners that had
made him healthy : he looked for the result of good
feeding in a powerful body, and for that of good
reading in a full strong mind.   Thus his pleasure
in the acquaintance of authors was rather in the
men and women themselves than in the merit of this
or that production.   To those who rose into sudden
notoriety this was especially agreeable ; they found
in him not so much an admirer of their writings

as a considerate and useful friend, and his good-humoured satire was often directed to cure what struck him as faults or misunderstanding of their position, as when to Miss Martineau, excusing herself from returning visits by her want of leisure and a carriage, he suggested that she should send an inferior authoress with her ear-trumpet in a hackney coach, to leave her cards about the town. He was, indeed, not given to severe censure, but could convey it under light words when he chose; thus when he checked the strong old-fashioned freedom of speech in Lord Melbourne by suggesting that 'they should assume everybody and everything to be damned, and come to the subject.' Mr. Rogers' curiously unworthy repugnance to being regarded as a man in business, provoked him to many a sharp bye-blow : looking one morning into a large display of royal invitations over the chimney-piece, he asked the company in a loud 'aside,' 'Does it not look as if the Bank had been accommodating the Duchess of Kent?' But by nature and by habit he was as tolerant of the faults of others as his keen perception permitted. I remember his saying with unusual earnestness : 'What a mystery is the folly and stupidity of the good !'

I have mentioned the independence of character

which secured him from moral injury in a society where the natural arrogance of aristocracy is fostered and encouraged by continual pressure and intrusion from without. He always showed the consciousness that he fully repaid any courtesy or condescension that he might receive by raising the coarser frivolity of high life to a level of something like intellectual enjoyment. Yet he could not altogether conceal his sense of the inevitable defects of idle opulence and rank without personal merit. I remember complaining to him one day of the insolence of some fine lady, and receiving a smart reproof for caring about such nonsense. 'You should remember that they are poodles fed upon cream and muffins, and the wonder is that they retain either temper or digestion.' For the active pursuit of wealth he had a far different estimate; he thought no man could be better employed than in making honest money: he said, 'he felt warmed by the very contact of such men as the great bankers and merchants of his time. He liked to bring home this satisfaction to his own personal position. 'What a blessing to have been born in this country, where three men, like my brothers and myself, starting from the common level of life, could, by the mere exercise of their own talents and industry, be what we are, with every material comfort and every requisite consideration.' Speaking of one of these, Mr. Robert Smith, the fine classic and distinguished Indian official, he burst forth : ' What a glorious possession for England that India is ! My brother Bobus comes to me one morning when I am in bed, and says he is going there, and wishes me good-bye. I turn round, go to sleep for some time, and when I wake, there he is again, standing by me, hardly at all altered, with a huge fortune.' His brother Courteney also returned from India with great wealth ; Sydney always spoke of him as a man of at least equal ability with himself. There was a current story that when some one alluded to the magnificent administration of Lord Hastings in India, he responded : ' Macnificent you mean.'

I am inclined to dwell somewhat on the clerical position of Mr. Sydney Smith, from the misapprehension concerning it that existed and still exists in the judgments of many estimable men. There can be no greater anachronism than to confound the estimates of the sacerdotal character as it has come to be regarded by public opinion in the first half of the nineteenth century, with the ancient standard that prevailed up to that period. The ministers of the Church of England, taken as a whole, were serious, not austere—pious, not devout—literary, not learned. Its prelates were, many of them, good scholars rather than theologians, and they rose to the Bench as often by an edition of a Greek play as by a commentary on the Scriptures. It is related by one, by no means the least eminent, that he dismissed his candidates for ordination with the injunction 'to improve their Greek, and not waste their time in visiting the poor.' His profession Mr. Sydney Smith went into young, without any notion of special aptitude, without any pretence of a spiritual vocation. He undertook to perform its duties in the different spheres in which they might be presented to him, to form his life on a certain basis of belief, to submit to its recognised restrictions, and to defer to its constituted authorities. If, besides these negative functions, he adorned the profession with learning or wit, if he strengthened its political constitution or advanced its intellectual interests, if, in a word, besides being a respectable clergyman, he became a man of mark in literature, or science, in social development or philanthropic work, he demanded that he should have his share of the dignities and wealth of the corporation to which

he belonged, and rise, if favoured by fortune and
sanctioned by desert, to the highest conditions of
the realm.   In this view of the ecclesiastical life
there was nothing strange or new; in fact, it was
strange and new to think otherwise.   The Church
of England, as the Church of Rome before it, par-
ticipated in all the intellectual as well as spiritual
movements of mankind, and did not shrink from
rights of interference in the government and policy
of the State.   It thought it no derogation to be a
valuable branch of the civil service, to guard the
morality and guide the education of the people.
It was, as a whole, pious not devout—literary not
learned—serious not austere.   Its best scholars
were classical rather than biblical; its most earnest
philanthropists and reformers were men of the
world.   Nor did it attempt to divest itself of political
objects and party bias.   It prided itself on its judicial attitude amid the passions of religious controversy, and if it had ejected the Nonconformists it had
cut itself off from the Nonjurors.   But in pure politics it was essentially Tory, and ecclesiastical advo-
cates of change and novelty were few and far between. Mr. Sydney Smith is therefore fully justified
in asserting the entire disinterestedness with which
he joined the Liberal camp, and in saying that ' it

12

would be indeed absurd to suppose that, in doing so, he had any thought or prospect of promotion in his profession.' But when, after many years of work and success in the advocacy of those opinions, and intimate connection with its political leaders, his party became predominant in the State, the apparent neglect of his services was at once a private wound and a public injury.

The Episcopate in this country brings with it not only a lofty social station, but an opportunity of that employment of the faculties which is most congenial to the mind of an intellectual Englishman —political distinction ; and for this Mr. Sydney Smith justly believed himself apt by nature and education. The peculiar combination of wit and good sense made his arguments accessible to every sincere mind—the lively enjoyed the one, and the dull were impressed with the other. But instead of being welcomed as a useful ally, and advanced to the posts in which he could wield his arms of clear conception, acute criticism, brilliant illustration, and searching satire, with power and satisfaction, he was treated as inconvenient if not superfluous. Lady Holland, indeed, recites, on some unknown authority, that Lord Grey, on taking possession of Downing Street, exclaimed: 'Now I can do

something for Sydney Smith!' but if there ever
was such an utterance, it ought rather to have been,
'Now I can find Sydney Smith something to do.'
But it is difficult to understand how, with one
sentiment or the other, so little was done for him.
In 1831, he was appointed to a Canonry of St.
Paul's, and in the hierarchy he rose no higher. I
heard Lord Melbourne say, 'Sydney Smith had
done more for the Whigs than all the clergy put
together, and our not making him a bishop was
mere cowardice.'

It was a natural feeling on the part of the
daughter to represent her father as treating the
neglect with dignified indifference, but neither his
conduct nor his language have left me with that
impression. Lord Brougham, indeed, told me that
when the Whig Government was formed, Mr.
Sydney Smith wrote to him to the effect that, as
for a Bishopric, it would not suit his friends to give
it him or him to receive it, but that he should be
glad of any other preferment,—and that he (Lord
Brougham) had answered him that 'in those expressions he had shown, as usual, his complete
common sense,' adding: 'Leave the fastnesses
of the Church to others; keep the snugnesses for
yourself.' I have no doubt Lord Brougham re-

ported his own words correctly; I am not so sure about those of Sydney Smith.

It is probable, however, that his own feelings on the matter swayed and changed with the temper of the moment. There were times, no doubt, when the sense of the comfort of the modest duties allotted to him was agreeable, as I remember in his salutation to a young Archdeacon, now, perhaps, the foremost Prelate in the Church : ' You have got your first honour in your profession—the first drippings of the coming shower. *I* have everything I want, a Canonry with excellent pasture, a charming parish and residence, and—what I will tell you privately, but it must not go any farther—an excellent living I never see.' This was Halliburton, near Exeter, which had been attached to his stall at Bristol. In the same state of mind he once expressed to me his feelings respecting the death of his eldest son at Oxford, in the full promise of the highest distinction : ' It was terrible at the time, but it has been best for me since ; it has been bad enough in life to have been ambitious for myself, it would have been dreadful to have been ambitious for another.'

The subject of his exclusion rarely occurs in his letters, but in one to Mrs. Grote (Dec. 1840), an-

nouncing the news of a batch of baronets, he anti-
cipates the honour for Mr. Grote (who, by the by,
afterwards refused a peerage), and adds : ' If he is
not, I will : the Ministers who would not make me a
bishop can't refuse to make me a baronet.' But
the real proof of the depth of injury inflicted by this
deprivation of the great privileges and powers of
his profession was his continual allusion and sharp,
though not malignant, satire against the Order. So
many instances crowd on the memory that selection
is not easy. I will mention those that first recur
to me, which are not already included in Lady Holland's ' Life.'

'I delight in a stage-coach and four, and how
could I have gone by one as a Bishop? I might
have found myself alone with a young lady of
strong dissenting principles, who would have called
for help, to disgrace the Church, or with an Atheist,
who told me what he had said in his heart, and
when I had taken refuge on the outside, I might
have found a Unitarian in the basket, or, if I
got on the box, the coachman might have told
me " he was once one of those rascally parsons,
but had now taken to a better and an honester
trade." '

' Why don't the thieves dress with aprons—so

convenient for storing any stolen goods? You would see the Archbishop of York taken off at every race-course, and not a prize-fight without an archdeacon in the paws of the police.'

'The Bishop of St. David's has been studying Welsh all the summer; it is a difficult language, and I hope he will be careful—it is so easy for him to take up the Funeral-Service, and read it over the next wedding-party, or to make a mistake in a tense in a Confirmation, and the children will have renounced their godfathers and godmothers, and got nothing in their place.'

'They now speak of the peculiar difficulties and restrictions of the Episcopal Office. I only read in Scripture of two inhibitions—boxing and polygamy.'

He was not likely to have much sympathy for the novel demand for the extension of Episcopacy in the colonies, which he called 'Colonial mitrophilism.' 'There soon will not be a rock in the sea on which a cormorant can perch, but they will put a Bishop beside it. Heligoland is already nominated.'

It will of course appear to many that the levity with which he would thus treat the dignitaries of his profession would of itself have unfitted him for its highest offices, and certainly with the present emotional and historical development of religious feeling in the Church, there would be much truth in the opinion. But this was not, and could not have been, his aspect of a hierarchy in which Swift had been a Dean and Sterne a Canon, not only without scandal but with popular admiration and national pride, and the objections to his elevation really apply quite as strongly to his status as a minister of the Church at all. The question may fairly be asked, why should he not have made quite as good a Bishop as he was a parish Priest and Canon of St. Paul's. The temperament which, in his own words, 'made him always live in the Present and the Future, and look on the Past as so much dirty linen,' was eminently favourable to his fit understanding and full accomplishment of whatever work he had to do. There has been no word of adverse criticism on his parochial administration, and he has left the best recollections of the diligence and scrupulous care with which he fulfilled his duties in connection with the Cathedral of St. Paul's.

He often spoke with much bitterness of the growing belief in three Sexes of Humanity—Men, Women, and Clergymen ; 'but, for his part, he would not surrender his rightful share of interference in

all the great human interests of his time.'   Had he
attained a seat on the Bench of Bishops, he would
assuredly have been considerate to his clergy, intelligent and active in all works of beneficence,
eminent in the work of education, and, what
is so rare in his profession, an excellent man
of business in all the temporal affairs of his diocese.
To the House of Lords, his union of lively perception and vigorous judgment would have been very
acceptable, and he would have arrested that
current of prejudiced opinion which would confine
the influence and interference of the members of
that Assembly, who have especially won their way
to its distinctions by their own various abilities,
to the discussion of purely professional topics.

But the development, as our century advanced,
of an ideal of the Church of England, in which first
the imaginative and spiritual elements, and later
the mystically-historical, came to supersede the
old moral, intellectual, and political order, not only
has tended to the exclusion from the hierarchy of
the very men who in the former time would have
been selected for its offices, but, during the latter
years of Mr. Sydney Smith's life, had so far taken
hold of the public mind that it was not uncommon
to hear, even from fair-judging men, a regret that

he had selected the clerical profession at all, and a secret repugnance to the fusion between what seemed to them the sacred and profane in his thoughts and language. The exclusion of the clergy from the ordinary amusements of English life was already gradually tending to their rarer appearance in general society, and the frequent presence of one of the body as a brilliant diner-out was becoming something anomalous. The constant growth of this feeling to the present time renders it difficult to many to understand how modern it was, and how rapid the change from the old-fashioned estimate of the manners and proprieties of clerical life. When Mr. Sydney Smith came to Yorkshire, he must still have found the sporting parson—a character now only lingering in the far-west of England—in full vigour; but it seems to have been distasteful to him, for when asked by Archbishop Harcourt (who had himself considerable sympathy with those diversions) whether he objected to seeing the clergy on horseback? he answered : ' Certainly not, provided they turn out their toes.' It is not uncharitable to attribute this special rigour in some degree to the entire absence of the sporting instinct in himself, which led him to regard ' being kicked up and down Pall Mall as a more reasonable exercise than riding

12*

a high-trotting horse,' and to confess that ' when he took a gun in hand he was sure that the safest position the pheasant could assume was just opposite its muzzle.'

It needs no argument to prove that susceptibilities on the score of irreverence increase in proportion to the prevalence of doubt and scepticism. When essential facts cease to be incontrovertible they are no longer safe from the humour of contrasts and analogies. It is thus that the secular use of scriptural allusion was more frequent in the days of simple belief in inspiration than in our times of linguistic and historical criticism. Phrases and figures were then taken as freely out of sacred as out of classical literature, and even characters as gross and ludicrous as some of Fielding's clergy were not looked upon as satire against the Church. Thus when Sydney Smith illustrated his objections to always living in the country by saying that ' he was in the position of the personage who, when he entered a village, straightway he found an ass,'—or described the future condition of Mr. Croker as ' disputing with the recording Angel as to the dates of his sins,'—or drew a picture of Sir George Cornewall Lewis in Hades, ' for ever and ever book-less, essay-less, pamphlet-less, grammar-

less, in vain imploring the Bishop of London, seated
aloft, for one little treatise on the Greek article—
-one smallest dissertation on the verb in μι,'—it
never occurred to him that he was doing anything
more than taking the most vivid and familiar images
as vehicles of his humour.   How little impropriety
he could have attached to these playfulnesses, is
evident from a striking passage in the ' Essay on
Wit,' which formed part of the series of Lectures
he delivered at the Royal Institution, and which
he was fond of describing ' as the most successful
swindle of the season.'

' It is a beautiful thing to observe the boundaries
which Nature has affixed to the ridiculous,
and to notice how soon it is swallowed up by
the more illustrious feelings of our nature ; ' and
after various powerful illustrations of this impression, he thus concludes :—' Who ever thinks of
turning into ridicule our great and ardent hope of
a world to come ?   Whenever the man of humour
meddles with these things, he is astonished to find
that in all the great feelings of their nature the
mass of mankind always think and act alike ;
that they are ready enough to laugh, but that they
are quite as ready to drive away with indignation
and contempt the light fool who comes with the

feather of wit to crumble the bulwarks of truth and
to beat down the temples of God.' *

There was another cause which at that time contributed to liberty on such points among serious
men—the absence of all religious controversy or
discussion in good society. When, in the decline
of his life, Mr. Luttrell took a tour of country-houses,
he told his friends on his return that he had found
himself quite put out by the theological talk that
prevailed in every house he had visited—except in
that perfect gentleman's, the Bishop of ——'s, where
the subject never occurred. This was in truth no
great exaggeration of the change that had taken
place in the public use of such topics, and would of
itself explain how Mr. Sydney Smith might to some
have appeared irreverent, while in fact the irreverence must to him have appeared all on the other
side. One of the main repugnancies of the churchmen of the early part of our century to what they
called ' Methodism '—that is, the great development of evangelical sentiment in English religion—
was the introduction into the open air of the world

---

* The most notorious, perhaps, of the scriptural allusions attributed
to Mr. Sydney Smith—the reply to Landseer's proposal to draw his
portrait : ' Is thy servant a dog, that he should do this thing ? ' was
really said by Mr. Lockhart.

of an order of thought and feeling which custom
had relegated to certain times and places, and
which it was neither good taste nor good sense to
make general and familiar. It was the boast and
tradition of the Church of England to take a '*Via
media*' in manner as in doctrine, which should keep
clear of lightness and of solemnity, of preciseness
and of passion. 'How beautiful it is,' I heard
Sydney Smith preach at Combe Florey, 'to see the
good man wearing the mantle of piety over the
dress of daily life—walking gaily among men, the
secret servant of God.' In this chance expression
it seemed to me, lay his main theory of religion.
In one of his admirable sermons (' On the Character
and Genius of the Christian Religion '), he says
emphatically : ' The Gospel has no enthusiasm—
it pursues always the same calm tenor of language,
and the same practical view, in what it enjoins. . . .
There is no other faith which is not degraded
by its ceremonies, its fables, its sensuality, or its
violence ; the Gospel only is natural, simple, correct,
and mild.' Another discourse has for its title, ' The
Pleasures of Religion,' on which he dilates with an
earnest conviction that it is not only possible to
make the best of both worlds, but that it is rather
for the daily contentment than for the extraordinary

solaces of life that Christianity has been given to mankind.

There is no doubt that his secular repute diminished to some extent the consideration that his powers as a preacher would otherwise have obtained. Though perhaps less carefully composed than his other writings, his Sermons abound with what is so rare in that form of literature—real interest; and while the subject-matter is level with an educated intelligence, the form adapts them to any mixed audience not solicitous for emotion or surprise. They are perhaps the foremost in that class of discourses, so difficult to find, which are suitable for a body of hearers neither private nor public enough for vivid appeals to the feelings or subtle demands on the understanding. His delivery was animated without being dramatic, and would recall to those familiar with his writings the sharp animadversion in one of his earliest productions—the small volumes printed in 1801, on the monotonous and conventional treatment of sacred subjects in the pulpit, but which, somehow or other, has had no place in his collected works—how undeservedly the following extracts would suffice to show:

'Why are we natural everywhere but in the pulpit?

No man expresses warm and animated feelings any-
where else with his mouth close, but with his whole
body ; he articulates with every limb, and talks from
head to foot with a thousand voices. Why this
holoplexia on sacred occasions alone ? Why call
in the aid of paralysis to piety ? Is it a rule of
oratory to balance the style against the subject,
and to handle the most sublime truths in the .
dullest language and the driest manner ? Is sin
to be taken from men, as Eve was from Adam,
by casting them into a deep slumber ? . . . We
have cherished contempt for centuries, and per-
severed in dignified tameness so long, that while
we are freezing common sense for large salaries in
stately churches, amidst whole acres and furlongs
of empty pews, the crowd are feasting on ungram-
matical fervour and illiterate animation in the
crumbling hovels of the Methodists.'

In considering the relation of Mr. Sydney
Smith's other works to his living reputation, it
seems difficult for the one to sustain and continue
the other unless by some combination of interest
in their subjects and their forms, and on this point
he shares the destiny and the difficulties of the
most eminent names in the history of British
letters. Should, indeed, a complete English educa-

tion ever become an object of serious study in this country, a great advantage and facility will be recognised in the circumstance that our best writers are more or less political. I do not allude to professed historians, or even to those who describe, attack, or defend the public affairs in which they have been personally engaged—such as Bacon, Milton, Clarendon, or Bolingbroke—but to the specially literary classes—the novelists and the divines—who have not been content to deal either with abstractions or theories, but have come down among their fellow-citizens to contend for any common cause that is agitating the nation. Hence there often seems a ludicrous disproportion between what seems the importance of the defence or attack and the weight of the defender or assailant. We might gladly commit the apology of the House of Hanover to the pellucid English of Addison's 'Freeholder,' or the less important party struggles of the Dukes of Grafton and Bedford to the rhetoric of the long-mysterious Junius; but we grudge the gigantic satire of Swift evoked by Wood's copper half-pence, and even the time of Walter Scott, devoted to the one-pound note of his country. But whether this be a waste of power or not, it seems to be so necessary a

product of our character and our institutions,
that when any powerful writer has the taste and
temperament of a politician, it is a wonder if he
be anything else. Thus it is fortunate that the
questions in which Mr. Sydney Smith lavished his
wit, were not only the topics of the day, but had
their roots in serious and permanent interests.

The Irish Church, which he so boldly satirised,
is abolished; the Ballot, which he ridiculed, is
established; the Ecclesiastical Commission, which
he was ready to oppose 'even to the loss of a portion of his own income and the whole of Dr. Spry's,'
is now the sole depository of the temporalities of
the Church, the 'Colonial' freedom he so early
advocated is complete; and if the Game-laws be
still on the statute-book, it is not from want of
criticism or objection. Thus whether his advocacy
succeeded or failed, it must not be forgotten that
these were matters which deeply agitated the
public mind of the England in which he lived, and
full account should be taken of the influence which
such a statesman of the study, armed with so
rare and well-tempered a glaive of wit, must have
exercised. But besides and beyond this marvellous
faculty, let no one despise the admirable vehicle of
language in which it is conveyed, or decline to join

in the adjuration he solemnly uttered : ' God preserve us the purity of style which from our earliest
days we have endeavoured to gather in the great
schools of ancient learning.'

VIII.

THE LAST DAYS OF HEINRICH HEINE.

THERE is no necessity to suppose any determined hostility, or the existence of either envy or malignity, in the repulsion with which ordinary minds shrink from the humouristic character. If to studious men it seems shallow, if to severe men it seems indifferent, if to pious men it seems irreverent, these are the inevitable consequences of their mental vision being brought to bear on objects it is not fitted to contemplate. The contrasts, the inconsistencies, the incongruities, which provoke and exercise the faculty of humour, are really invisible to most persons, or, when perceived, arouse a totally distinct order of ideas and associations. It must seem to them at best a mischievous inclination to find a source of mirth in the sufferings, and struggles, and troubles of others; and when the humourist extends this practice to himself, and discovers a certain satisfaction in his own weaknesses and miseries, introverting the very sensations of pleasure and pain, he not only checks the sympathy he might otherwise have won, but his very courage is . interpreted into an unnatural audacity, alike defiant of the will of Heaven and of the aid of man.   The deep consolations of this faculty in the trials and extremities of life are altogether unknown to them ; and it is only when such a man as Heinrich Heine has passed away— when the bold handling of men and things by the implacable humourist can offend no more—that a merciful judgment can be expected for a character which contained many elements of moral greatness, and for a just appreciation of those rare talents which gave glory to his youth, and did not desert him in the bitterest sufferings of his maturity.

Never, indeed, did a volume of verse receive a more general and immediate welcome than did the 'Buch der Lieder' in Germany.   The most conventional classes were not proof against the charm of its simplicity and truth ; old statesmen, like Gentz, who in the abstract would have liked to have shut up the young republican in a fortress, spoke of the book as giving them an 'Indian summer of pleasure and passion ;' philosophers, to whom such doctrine as they found there seemed wholly sensuous, and theologians to whom some light treatment of serious matter was naturally painful, were subdued by the grace of the youth who stood ready to take the throne the ancient Goethe was about to leave, and were glad to attribute the errors they lamented to the circumstances of his family life and to the effervescence of his fresh imagination.

Between those productions and his last work lay many eventful years, but less difference in the characteristics of the author than he himself was wont to imagine. He frequently spoke of his early writings with a regretful tenderness, as of a happy world now lost to view ; but the critic may remark that there is no stamp of mind so indelible as that of - the poetic humourist, and that where those powers once vigorously coexist no changes or chances can divorce them altogether. There may be no palpable humour in Thomas Hood's ' Song of the Shirt,' or ' Bridge of Sighs,' and yet we feel that these poems are the expression of the gay common sense of his earlier mind refined into the most solemn pathos by the contemplation of the sorrows of humanity. Thus, too, in the retrospect of Heine's inner self, the voice that comes from the bed of long sickness and approaching death is the very same that trolled out those delightful melodies that every boy and woman in Germany knows by heart.

Above all literary characters of our time, Heine had throughout the calamity of a false position. With so acute a sense of classical forms and antique grace as to make him often well content to live

A Pagan suckled in a creed out-worn,

he was regarded as a chief of the Romantic school; with a genial and pleasure-loving temperament, he was mortified by physical infirmity and moral disappointment into a harsh and sometimes cruel satirist; with a deep religious sentiment, and even narrow theological system, he was thrust into the chair of an apostle of scepticism; with no clear political convictions or care for theories of government, he had to bear all the pains and penalties of political exile, the exclusion from the commerce of the society he best enjoyed, and the inclusion among men from whom he shrank with an instinctive dislike. The immediate cause of his banishment from Germany has never been clearly stated. He does not seem to have been the object of any particular prosecution, but he had made himself sufficiently obnoxious to the authorities to make his existence in Germany insecure.

When questioned in France as to his nationality, he used to call himself *Prussien libéré*, and he writes that he had been haunted with unpleasant visions, 'had seen himself in the attitude of Prometheus, and had fancied the sun turned into a Prussian cockade.' A high legal functionary had also told him 'that Spandau was very cold in winter; that no oysters came there, so far from the sea; and that the inhabitants caught no game, except the flies which fell into the soup;' so on May 1, 1831, he betook himself to the fatherland of Champagne and the Marseillaise. From this time forward, we see him doing all he can to make himself a Frenchman, but without success. There is always an old-German—we would say, notwithstanding all his anti-Anglicanism, English humour—which stands between him and the French mind with its clear wit and its hard logic. But the ingenuity, the readiness, above all the gaiety, of the Parisians, seemed to him almost a necessity of existence, for which his temperament had hitherto yearned in vain: it was not the old Greek life, but it was something like it, in its open-air liveliness, its alert passage from thought to thought, its keen relish of sensual pleasure.

In contrast to this, therefore, his impressions of

England, which he visited shortly after, were pro-
portionably disagreeable. London struck him
mightily 'like the stroke of a cudgel over his
shoulders ;' and he found in the astonishment of
the waiter at the Piazza Coffee-house, when he
asked him to bring him for breakfast one of the fine
cauliflowers he saw below him, a type of the horror with which we regard any deviation from our
national manners. He called us a country 'where
all the machines moved like men, and all the men
so like machines, that he was continually looking
to discover where they were wound up ;' and even
in his latter days, when calmer judgment and some
relations of personal affection had made him recant
much of his distaste to us, he still suggested that
'Bria, or Britinia, the White Island of Scandi-
navian mythology, to which the souls of the heroes
were transported after death, was nothing more
nor less than that Albion which even now looks so
very dead-alive to all strangers.' *

An historical incident of the Bonaparte dynasty,
in connection with his private life, had singularly
affected his boyish fancy. The Grand-Duchy of
Berg, of which Dusseldorf (his birthplace) was the

---

* He said to me in 1840 'I must revisit England, if only to judge
and understand you better.'

capital, passed from the possession of the Elector Palatine to that of Bavaria, and thence was unceremoniously transferred to the dominion of General Murat in exchange for the Bavarian Tyrol, which Napoleon had wrested from the empire of Austria. But in those days advancement was rapid, and the Grand-Duke of Berg becoming king of Naples, abdicated his duchy in favour of the eldest son of Louis king of Holland. 'Thus,' writes Heine in 1854, 'Louis Napoleon, who never abdicated, is my legitimate sovereign.'

It was there the boy saw 'Him—the Emperor.'

'The Emperor, with his *cortége*, rode straight down the avenue of the Hofgarten at Dusseldorf, notwithstanding the police regulations that no one should ride down the avenue under the penalty of a fine of five dollars. The Emperor, in his invisible green uniform, and his little world-renowned hat, sat on his white charger, carelessly, almost lazily, holding the rein with one hand, and with the other good-naturedly patting the neck of the horse. It was a sunny marble hand, one of the two which had bound fast the many-headed monster of anarchy to pacify the war of races, and it good-naturedly patted the neck of the horse. The face, too, of the hue which we find in the

18

marble busts of Greeks and Romans, the features
as finely proportioned as in antiques, and a smile
on the lips warming and tranquillising every heart,
while we knew that those lips had but to whistle *et
la Prusse n'existait plus*, and to whistle again and
all the Holy Roman Empire would have danced
before him. The brow was not so clear, for the
spectres of future conflicts were cowering here ;
and there were the creative thoughts, the huge
seven-mile-boot thoughts, in which the spirit of
the Emperor strode invisibly over the world, every
one of which thoughts would have given a German
author full materials to write about all the rest of
his natural life.'

Though these phrases now read as a weird
irony of romance, yet, if the enthusiasm of Heine
had been confined to pleasant images like these,
he would only have asserted a poet's privilege ; but
there is too much ill-will to others mixed up with
this hero-worship to allow it to be so simply vindicated. His relation to that marvellous people—of
whom Goethe has somewhere said, that 'Providence committed to their care the moral law of the
world, not because they were better or wiser than
others, but because they were more obstinate and
persistent—' not only alienated him from the na-

tional cause of Germany, but gave him a vindictive gratification in its discomfiture : he enjoyed the very tempest which had brought down the pride of German States almost to a level with the dependence and insignificance of his own race, just as in later years he directed his bitterest irony against ' the slaves who had been let loose in the peril of the storm to work the pumps, and draw the cables and risk their lives, but who, when the good ship floated safe once more, were turned back into the hold and chained nicely down again in political darkness.' Thus, the poem of ' Deutschland' is the one of his works where his humour runs over into the coarsest satire, and the malice can only be excused by the remembrance that he too had been exposed to some of the evil influences of a servile condition.

Among these, no doubt, may be reckoned the position of a man of commercial origin and literary occupation in his relation to the upper order of society in the northern parts of Germany. There the high mental cultivation and reflective character of the youth of the middle and lower classes contrasts dangerously with the almost exclusive military tastes of the nobility. The arrogance engendered by the continual exercise of Man as a mere mechanical agent, and by the habit of regarding physical force as the main legitimate instrument of authority, is there unsupported by that predominant wealth and ancient territorial possession which give the strength of prescription even to a questionable assumption of command. Here there remained, and after all the events of the last year there still remains, sufficient element of discontent to justify the recorded expression of a philosophic German statesman, ' that in Prussia the war of classes had still to be '' fought out." ' And this in truth was the mainspring of Heine's radicalism. This made him delight even in the system which preached equality under the sword, and in which every peasant felt that though not a freeman he might become a king. This it was which made him unable to comprehend the far different condition and popular associations of British aristocracy, and made him write that he grudged not the eighteen-pence he paid to see Westminster Abbey, ' for he saw there that the great of the earth were not immortal, and told the verger he was delighted with his exhibition, but would willingly have paid as much again if he could have seen that collection complete; for as long as the aristocrats of England are not gathered to their fathers, as long as the collection at West-minster is not complete, so long remains undecided the battle between Birth and the People, and the alliance between England and French citizenship, unstable and insecure.'

And yet it was in the Parliamentary Government of France that Heine found the only real political satisfaction expressed in his writings. The two last volumes of his Miscellaneous Works contain the letters he furnished to the 'Augsburg Gazette' from 1840 to 1844, in the character of 'our own correspondent.' This kind of republication is rarely interesting, whatever amount of ability it displays. The best periodical writing, from its nature, is bound up with the interests and passions of the hour and ought to occupy itself with the future little, if at all; and if by chance such a book falls into our hands, we usually read it with a mournful, and it may be a malicious, gratification at the exaggeration of its suppositions, the falsity of its predictions, the now-revealed folly of much of the sententious wisdom it enunciates. The salt, therefore, that keeps productions of this nature fresh must indeed be genuine, and the justice of Heine's views is sufficiently established by subsequent events to entitle the political opinions of their author, though a poet and a wit, to some respect, and to except this revival from the ordinary rules of decent literary interment. For although gift of prevision in public matters is, perhaps, but the perfection of common sense, yet, somehow or other, it is the quality least apparent in men holding high political station. It seems to be a sad necessity that the so-called practical men are limited to the knowledge of the time that is slipping away beneath their feet, and that the man who sees far ahead is rarely permitted to provide against the coming evil or to improve the nascent good. Thus it may be nothing but a singular coincidence that the Duke of Orleans in February 1840 appeared to Heine to have the aspect of a man anticipating a terrible catastrophe, and earnestly desiring a war that he might rather perish in the clear waters of the Rhine, than in the gutters of Paris; but there is something more in the foresight which, in December 1841, denounced in France the dissolution of the ties of common thought and principle, that extinction of *esprit de corps* which constitutes the moral death of a people, that absorption of material interests, which one fine day would permit a second 18th Brumaire to overthrow the *bourgeoisie*, a second Directory, and to establish the government of the sword with its din of glory, its stench of dying lamps, its rounds of cannon *en permanence*. Thus again, in 1842, he discerns in the coming time a mixed odour of blood and Russia-leather, which makes him express a hope that the next generation may come into the world with backs strong enough to bear all that Fate prepares for them.

But there is one image of the future which exercises over him a terrible fascination, disturbing the clearness of his vision, as it has done that of so many others. When he speaks of Communism, he is as panic-stricken as were the authors of the 'Esclave Vindex,' and the 'Spectre Rouge,' and as still are the higher and middle classes of France after their terrible experience, and then cannot get out of his head that the Socialists are the Masters of the approaching world. With horror he looks forward to the rule of those sombre iconoclasts, 'whose horny hands will break to pieces the idols of beauty he loves so well, will tear down all the pleasant frivolities of art, and pluck up the laurel-trees to plant potatoes in their stead.' He mourns for the lilies that neither toiled nor spun and yet were dressed so gloriously, and who now will be torn from the ground ; for the roses, the leisurely lovers of the nightingales, those unprofitable singers who cannot be allowed any longer to occupy time or space;' and above all for the 'book of songs,' 'which now only the grocer will use to hold the coffee and the snuff of the ancient females of the years to be;' and he attempts in vain to console himself by the reflection that the old society must perish because it is a whited sepulchre, and that those good old women will then have the aforesaid luxuries, which our present institutions deny them. That this logical conclusion is a poor satisfaction continually breaks out, especially in the sincerity of his verse, where it is apparent how distasteful to him is that equality from below which he imperatively requires from above. In truth Heine was no sincere democrat, as the colleagues of his political youth found out and bitterly resented. The quarrel deepened on both sides; Börne and the German Republicans denounced him as an apostate, and he retaliated by fierce ridicule and disclosures of confidential relations and private affairs which no party differences can justify. In verses, too, such as these, he insolently sank his imagined recantation:

> Alas! for the moth that has burnt his wings,
> And sank to the rank of creeping things;
> In foreign dust with creatures to crawl,
> That smell so strong, tho' they be so small;

The vermin-comrades that I must swallow,
Because in the self-same mire I wallow :
As Virgil's Scholar of old knew well,
The Poet of Exile—the Poet of Hell ;

With agony I review the time
When I hummed at home my wingèd rhyme,
And swung on the edge of a broad sun-flower
In the air and smoke of a German bower.

Roses were not too good for me,
I sipped them like the genteelest bee,
And high-born butterflies shared my lot,
And the Artist—the grasshopper—shunned me not.

But my wings are scorched—and I murmur in vain,
I shall see my Father-land never again ;
A worm I live, and a worm I die
In the far-away filth of a foreign sty.

I would to God I had never met
That water-fly,—that blue coquette,
With her winning ways and wanton *taille*,
The fair, the fair—the false *Canaille.*'

Another graver poem represents a more wholesome state of mind, and sums up with a manly
sorrow those feelings which, I fear, are common
to all men of poetic sensibility who deal with the
coarser motives and meaner objects that influence
public affairs.

In Freedom's War, of ' Thirty years ' and more,
  A lonely outpost have I held—in vain :
With no triumphant hope or prize in store,
  Without a thought to see my home again.

13*

I watched both day and night : I could not sleep
   Like my well-tented comrades far behind,
Though near enough to let their snoring keep
   A friend awake, if e'er to doze inclined.

And thus, when solitude my spirits shook,
   Or fear, for all but fools know fear sometimes,
To rouse myself and them, I piped and took
   A gay revenge in all my wanton rhymes.

Yes ! there I stood—my musket always ready,
   And when some sneaking rascal showed his head,
My eye was vigilant, my aim was steady,
   And gave his brains an extra dose of lead.

But war and justice have far different laws,
   And worthless acts are often done right well ;
The rascals' shots were better than their cause,
   And I was hit—and hit again, and fell !

That outpost is abandoned : while the one
   Lies in the dust, the rest in troops depart ;
Unconquered—I have done what could be done,
   With sword unbroken, and with broken heart.

When the palaces of Louis-Philippe were plundered in the revolution of 1848, the names of persons who received pensions from the civil list were published, and among others Heine was set down for two hundred pounds per annum. It may be imagined with what glee this intelligence was received by the enemies of Heine. His reaction was thus explained : he had been all along the paid advocate of the Orleans government, and his retirement from the world about this time, from quite another cause, was attributed to his sense of the disgrace. But in truth there was nothing in the revelation to injure the character of the recipient or of the donor. M. Thiers was much attracted by the literary German, who was more lively and witty than the Frenchmen who surrounded him, and Heine was delighted with the Frenchman, in comparison with whose vivacity and agility of mind all other Frenchmen seemed to him little better than clumsy Germans. Heine took the money, which enabled him at his ease to defend the cause he approved and the men he liked, and contrived to combine fidelity to his friends with independence of spirit.

By the side of the political conflict that was ever going on in the mind of Heine was one of a deeper and more important character, to which I have already alluded. Speaking of Shakspeare in one of his earlier works, he describes him as being at once both Greek and Hebrew, and admires how in him the spiritual and the artistic faculties are so thoroughly amalgamated as to produce the completest development of the human nature. In making this observation, he was no doubt conscious of the unceasing warfare of those moral elements within himself, and of his difficulty to combine or reconcile them. He must have seen, too, as clearly as those about him, how these impressions were affected by his temperament and circumstances. In his gay health and pleasant Parisian days the old gods haunted and enchanted him, like the legendary Tannhauser in the Venus-Mountain, while in his hours of depression, and above all in the miserable sufferings of his later life, the true religious feeling of his hereditary faith mastered, awed, and yet consoled him.

The singular charm which the old Hellenic mythology exercises over certain minds is something quite separate from antiquarian interest or even classical learning. The little Latin and the no Greek which our poet Keats acquired at his Enfield seminary and in his study of Lemprière, seem a very inadequate source for the vivid, almost personal, affection with which gods and goddesses,

> Not yet dead,
> But in old marbles ever beautiful,

inspired the author of Endymion and Hyperion. The sentiment, indeed, which produced and sustained the ancient religion was something very different from the modern reproduction ; yet such

examples as Keats and Heine attest the power of
the appeal which Grecian genius made once and
for ever to the sensuous imaginations of mankind,
and which all the influences of our positive and
demure civilisation protest against in vain. But
while the English poet yearned for that happy
supernatural society with all the ardour of boyish
passion, with Heine the feeling is rather that of a
regretful tenderness, mourning over a delightful
phase of human superstition, which he knows can
never return, but which in his mind is ever contrasting itself with the gravity of the religion of
sorrow and with piety divorced from pleasure.
Like the entranced traveller of Italian story, he
continually saw the exiled Olympians pass by him
in divine distress, the milk-white oxen garlanded
with withered leaves, and the children running with
extinguished torches.

The intellectual disposition of Heine was so
averse to that habit of philosophical speculation
which has occupied, and even contented, the cultivated Germans under their disastrous politics
and the deficiencies of their social system, that
there may be little to regret in the loss of the
work on Hegel, which Heine asserts that he sacrificed to his growing sense of personal religion;

nor is it easy to represent to one's self the picture
of Heine at twenty-two, sentimentally contempla-
ting the stars as the abodes of the blest, and of
Hegel scornfully depicting them as 'spots on the
face of heaven.'   But in February 1848—in the
very paroxysm of France—Heine was struck
down by a fatal malady, during which the more
serious elements of his character were necessarily
brought to view.   While in all but constant darkness, he thought, and listened, and dictated, preserving to the last his clearness of intellect, his
precision of diction, and his invincible humour.

I had made his acquaintance in 1840, when
he was apparently in robust health and a brilliant
member of the society of *Frondeurs* against the
Government of King Louis-Philippe, of which the
intellectual leader was George Sand, and the
political the Abbé Lamennais.   It was at that
time that the latter was imprudently prosecuted
for the tract 'De l'Esclavage Moderne,' which would
have been regarded with us as a very harmless
diatribe, and sentenced to several months' imprison-
ment.   I remember Heine expressing to the con-
demned politician the fear that the confinement
might be injurious to his health, and the Abbé's
reply, ' Mon enfant, il manque toujours quelque

chose à la belle vie, qui ne finit pas sur le champ
de bataille, sur l'échafaud, ou en prison.' Happy
would it have been for the Poet if any such destiny
had awaited him as attends the soldier or the
martyr! He had long ago drawn a picture of the
old age he aspired to attain,—age retaining the
virtues of youth, its unselfish zeal, its unselfish
tears. 'Let me become an old man, still loving
youth, still, in spite of the feebleness of years,
sharing in its gambols and in its dangers; let my
voice tremble and weaken as it may, while the
sense of the words it utters remains fresh with
hope, and unpalsied by fear.' Piteously different
was this vision from the reality which found its true
expression in the following apologue, and in the
poems which form the best illustration of the
power of genius to draw up treasure from the
deepest abysses of human calamity.

'I will cite you a passage from the Chronicle of
Limburg. This chronicle is very interesting for
those who desire information about the manners
and customs of the Middle Ages in Germany. It
describes, like a Journal des Modes, the costumes
both of men and women as they came out at the
time. It gives also notices of the songs which
were piped and sung about each year, and the

first lines of many a love-ditty of the day are
there preserved. Thus, in speaking of A.D. 1480,
it mentions that in that year through the whole
of Germany songs were piped and sung, sweeter
and lovelier than all the measures hitherto known
in German lands, and that young and old—
especially the ladies—went so mad about them,
that they were heard to sing them from morning
to night. Now these songs, the chronicle goes on
to say, were written by a young clerk, who was
affected by leprosy, and who dwelt in a secret
hermitage apart from all the world. You know,
dear reader, assuredly what an awful malady in
the Middle Ages this leprosy was; and how the
poor creatures who fell under this incurable calamity were driven out of all civil society, and
allowed to come near no human being. Dead-
alive, they wandered forth wrapt up from head to
foot, the hood drawn over the face, and carrying in
the hand a kind of rattle called the Lazarus-
clapper, by which they announced their presence, so that every one might get out of their
way in time. This poor clerk, of whose fame
as poet and songster this Chronicle of Limburg
has spoken, was just such a leper, and he sat
desolate, in the solitude of his sorrow, while all

Germany, joyful and jubilant, sang and piped his songs.

'Many a time in the mournful visions of my nights, I think I see before me the poor clerk of the Chronicle of Limburg, my brother in Apollo, and his sad, suffering eyes stare strangely at me from under his hood; but at the same moment he seems to vanish, and clanging through the distance, like the echo of a dream, I hear the sharp rattle of the Lazarus-clapper.'

And, as it were in the person of this unfortunate being, he entitles the following poems 'Lazarus.'

I

Leave those sacred parables,
  Leave those views of true devotion,
Show me kernels in the shells,
  Show me truth within the notion.

Show me why the Holiest one
  Sinks by man's insane resentment,
While the vile centurion
  Prances on in proud contentment.

Where the fault? By whom was sent
  The evil no one can relieve?
Jehovah not omnipotent!
  Ah! that I never will believe.

And so we go on asking, till
  One fine morning lumps of clay
Stop our mouths for good or ill;
  That's no answer—still I say.

II

My one love is the Dark Ladie;
  O she has loved me long and well;
Her tears, when last she wept o'er me,
  Turned my hair grey, where'er they fell.

She kissed my eyes, and all was black,
  Embraced my knees, and both were lame,
Clung to my neck, and from my back
  The marrow to her kisses came.

My body is a carcass, where
  The spirit suffers prison-bound:
Sometimes it tosses in despair,
  And rages like a crazy hound.

Unmeaning curses ! oath on oath
  Cannot destroy a single fly :
Bear what God sends you—nothing loth
  To pray for better by and by.

III

Old Time is lame and halt,
  The snail can barely crawl :
But how should I find fault
  Who cannot move at all !

No gleam of cheerful sun !
  No hope my life to save !
I have two rooms, the one
  I die in and the grave.

May be, I've long been dead,
  May be, a giddy train
Of phantoms fills my head,
  And haunts what was my brain.

These dear old gods or devils,
  Who see me stiff and dull,
May like to dance their revels
  In a dead Poet's skull.

Their rage of weird delight
  Is luscious pain to me :
And my bony fingers write
  What daylight must not see.

IV

What lovely blossoms on each side
  Of my youth's journey shone neglected ;
Left by my indolence or pride
  To waste unheeded or respected !

Now, when I scent the coming grave,
  Here, where I linger sick to death,
There flowers ironically wave
  And breathe a cruel luscious breath.

One violet burns with purple fire,
  And sends its perfume to my brain :
To think I had but to desire,
  And on my breast the prize had lain !

O Lethe ! Lethe ! thanks to Heaven,
  That your black waves for ever flow ;
Thou best of balsams ! freely given
  To all our folly and our woe.

V

I saw them smile, I heard them prattle,—
  I watched them pass away :
Their tears, life-struggle, and death-rattle,
  Scarcely disturbed my day.

I followed coffin after coffin,
　In different moods of mind,
Sometimes regretting, sometimes scoffing,
　And then went home and dined.

Now sudden passionate remembrance
　Flames up within my heart ;—
The dead are dead, but from their semblance
　I cannot bear to part.

And most one tearful recollection
　Besets me, till it grows
Far wilder than the old affection
　From whose decay it rose.

A colourless, a ghastly blossom,
　She haunts my fevered nights,
And seems to ask my panting bosom
　For posthumous delights.

Dear phantom ! closer, closer, press me :
　Let dead and dying meet :
Hold by me,—utterly possess me,
　And make extinction sweet.

VI

You were a fair young lady, with an air
Gentle, refined, discreet and debonnaire ;—
I watched, and watched in vain, to see when first
The passion-flower from your young heart would burst :—

Burst into consciousness of loftier things
Than reason reckons or reflection brings, —
Things that the prosy world lets run to seed,
But for which women weep and brave men bleed.

Can you remember when we strolled together,
Through the Rhine vineyards, in gay summer weather ?

Outlaughed the sun, and every genial flower
Shared the serene emotion of the hour.

In many a hue the roses blushed to please,
The thick carnations kissed the morning breeze;
The very daisies' unpretending show
Seemed into rich ideal life to blow.

While you in quiet grace walked by my side,
Dressed in white satin, that might suit a bride,
But like some little maid of Netscher's limning,
Your untried heart well hid beneath the trimming.

VII

My cause at Reason's bar was heard,—
  'Your fame is clear as noon-day's sun'—
The sentence ran,—' by deed or word
  The fair accused no ill has done.'

Yes ! while my soul was passion-torn,
  She dumb and motionless stood by ;
She did not scoff, she did not scorn,
  Yet 'guilty, guilty,' still I cry.

For an accusing Voice is heard,
  When night is still and thought is dim,
Saying, ' It was not deed or word,
  But her bad heart, that ruined him.'

Then come the witnesses and proofs,
  And documents of priceless cost ;
But when the dawn has touched the roofs,
  All vanish, and my cause is lost :

And in my being's darkest deep
  The plaintiff seeks the shame to hide :
One sense—one memory—will not sleep—
  That I am utterly destroyed !

VIII.

My fathomless despair to show
  By certain signs, your letter came:
  A lightning-flash, whose sudden flame
Lit up th' abyss that yawned below.

What! you by sympathies controlled!
  You, who in all my life's confusion,
  Stood by me, in your self-seclusion,
As fair as marble, and as cold.

O God! how wretched I must be!
  When even *she* begins to speak;
  When tears run down that icy cheek,
The very stones can pity me.

There's something shocks me in her woe:
  But if that rigid heart is rent,
  May not the Omnipotent relent,
And let this poor existence go.

IX

The Sphynx was all a Woman: proof
  I cannot give you, but I know it;
The lion's body, tail, and hoof,
  Are but the nonsense of the poet.

And this real Sphynx, to madden us,
  Goes on propounding her enigma,
Just as she tortured Œdipus
  With all his sad domestic stigma.

How fortunate she does not know
  Herself her secret's mystic thunder!
If once she spoke the word, the blow
  Would split the world itself asunder.

x

Three hags on a seat
 Where the cross-roads meet ?
They mumble and grin,
They sigh and they spin :
Great ladies they be,
Though frightful to see.

One moistens the thread
   In her pendulous mouth,
And the distaff is fed
   Though her lip has the drought.

One dances the spindle
   In fanciful ways,
Till the sparks from it kindle
   Her eyes to a blaze.

The third holds the shears
   The discussion to close :
While with voice hard and dreary
She sings ' Miserere,'
And the rheum of her tears
   Makes warts on her nose.

Sweet Fate ! prithee answer
   My love with your knife ;—
And cut out this cancer
   Of damnable life.

XI

I long not for Elysian fields
Or Paradise, or lands of bliss,
No fairer forms that region yields
Than in my time, I've known in this.

No Angel with the softest wing
Can be to me the wife I lose,
And on the clouds to sit and sing
Is not a pastime I should choose.

Dear Lord! how I should bless Thy name
If Thou, instead of Heaven, would'st please
To mend this body's ragged frame,
And give just gold enough for ease.

I know that sin and vice abound,
But it has been my wont for years
To pace unharmed this naughty ground
And loiter through this vale of tears.

Little I heed the noisy town ;
Seldom I pass my humble door ;
In slippers and in dressing-gown
I rest, and ask for nothing more,

Except my wife ; whene'er she speaks,
My soul no other music needs ;
And in her honest eye it seeks
The secret of all noble deeds.

A little health, a little wealth
Are all I pray for, let us go
Through a long life of happy stealth,
I and my wife *in statu quo.*

During these years of misery I had no opportunity of visiting Heine, but soon after his death
I received a letter from a lady to whom I applied
for information concerning him, and which seems
to me so faithful and pathetic a picture of this

great agony that I am grateful to be permitted
by her representatives to insert it here. I would
not have done so were she still living, for, with
all the talent of expression which has already
made many of her personal experiences on matters
of interest to others known to the world, she
would have been seriously annoyed at any public
reference to the noble and delightful qualities
which have left so deep an impression on all who
knew her.

'My husband tells me that you wish to have
my recollections of poor Heine when I last saw
him. I had known him above twenty years ago
as a child of eleven or twelve at Boulogne, where
I sat next him at a table d'hôte. He was then a
fat, short, man; shortsighted, and with a sensual
mouth. He heard me speak German to my
mother, and soon began to talk to me, and then
said, "When you go to England you can tell your
friends that you have seen Heinrich Heine." I
replied, "And who is Heinrich Heine?" He
laughed heartily, and took no offence at my
ignorance, and we used to lounge on the end of
the pier together, where he told me stories in
which fish, mermaids, watersprites, and a very
funny old French fiddler with a poodle, who was

14

diligently taking three sea baths a day, were mixed up in the most fanciful manner, sometimes humorous, and very often pathetic, especially when the watersprites brought him German greetings from the " Nord See."

‘ He since told me that the poem—

> Wenn ich an deinem Hause
> Am Morgen vorüber geh,
> So freut's mich, du liebe Kleine,
> Wenn ich dich am Fenster seh, &c.

was meant for me and my " braune Augen."

‘ He was at Boulogne a month or two, and I saw him often then, and always remembered with great tenderness the poet who had told me the beautiful stories, and been so kind to me, and so sarcastic to every one else.

‘ I never saw him again till I went to Paris three years ago, when I heard that he was dying and very poor. I sent my name and a message that if he chanced to remember the little girl to whom he told " Mährchen " years ago at Boulogne, I should like to see him. He sent for me directly, remembered every little incident, and all the people who were in the same inn; a ballad I had sung, which recounted the tragical fate of Ladye

Alice and her humble lover, Giles Collins, and ended by Ladye Alice taking only one spoonful of the gruel, "With sugar and spices so rich," while after her decease, "The parson licked up the rest." This diverted Heine extremely, and he asked after the parson who drank the gruel directly.

'I for my part could hardly speak to him, so shocked was I by his appearance. He lay on a pile of mattresses, his body wasted so that it seemed no bigger than a child under the sheet which covered him—the eyes closed, and the face altogether like the most painful and wasted "Ecce Homo" ever painted by some old German painter.

'His voice was very weak and I was astonished at the animation with which he talked—evidently his mind had wholly survived his body. He raised his powerless eyelids with his thin white fingers, and exclaimed, "Gott! die kleine Lucie ist gross geworden und hat einen Mann; das ist eigen!" He then earnestly asked if I was happy and contented, and begged me to bring my husband to see him. He said again he hoped I was happy now as I had always been such a merry child. I answered that I was no longer so merry as the

kleine Lucie had been, but very happy and contented, and he said, " Das ist schön ; es bekommt
Einem gut eine Frau zu sehen, die kein wundes
Herz herum trägt, um es von allerlei Männern
ausbessern zu lassen, wie die Weiber hier zu Lande,
die es am Ende nicht merken, dass was ihnen
eigentlich fehlt ist gerade dass sie gar keine
Herzen haben." I took my husband to see him,
and we bid him good-bye. He said that he hoped
to see me again—ill as he was, he should not die
yet.

'Last September I went to Paris again, and
found Heine removed, and living in the same
street as myself in the Champs-Elysées ; I sent
him word I was come, and soon received a note
painfully written in pencil by him as follows :—

" Hochgeehrte grossbritannische Göttinn Lucie !
—Ich liess durch den Bedienten zurückmelden,
dass ich mit Ausnahme des letzten Mitwochs alle
Tage und zu jeder beliebigen Stunde bereit sey,
your Godship bey mir zu empfangen. Aber ich
habe bis heute vergebens auf solcher himmlischen
Erscheinung gewartet. Ne tardez plus de venir !
Venez aujourd'hui, venez demain, venez souvent.
Vous demeurez si près de moi, dem armen Schatten
in den Elisäischen Feldern !

" Lassen Sie mich nicht zu lange warten. Anbey schicke ich Ihnen die 4 ersten Bände der Franzö-sischen Ausgabe meiner unglückseligen Werke.

" Unterdessen verharre ich Ihrer Göttlichkeit

" Unterthänigster und ergebenster Anbeter,

" HEINRICH HEINE.

" P.S. The parson drank the gruel water."

' I went immediately, and climbed up five stories to a small room, where I found him still on the same pile of mattresses on which I had left him three years before; more ill he could not look, for he looked dead already, and wasted to a shadow. When I kissed him, his beard felt like swandown or a baby's hair, so weak had it grown, and his face seemed to me to have gained a certain beauty from pain and suffering. He was very affectionate to me and said, " Ich habe jetzt mit der ganzen Welt Frie-den gemacht, und endlich auch mit dem lieben Gott, der schickt mir dich nun als schöner Todesen-gel; gewiss sterb' ich bald." I said, " Armer Dich-ter, bleiben Ihnen noch immer so viele herrliche Illusionen, dass Sie. eine reisende Engländerin für Azrael ansehen können ? Das war sonst nicht der Fall, Sie konnten uns ja nicht leiden." He answered, " Ja, mein Gott, ich weiss doch gar nicht was ich gegen die Engländer hatte, dass ich immer so boshaft gegen sie war, es war aber wahrlich nur Muthwillen, eigentlich hasste ich sie nie, und ich habe sie auch nie gekannt. Ich war einmal in England vor langen Jahren, kannte aber niemand, und fand London recht traurig und die Leute auf der Strasse kamen mir unausstehlich vor. Aber England hat sich schön gerächt, sie schickte mir ganz vorzügliche Freunde—dich, und Milnes—der gute Milnes, und noch mehrere."

‘ I saw him two or three times a week during a two months' stay in Paris, and found him always full of lively conversation and interest in everything, and of his old undisguised vanity, pleased to receive bad translations of his works, and anxious beyond measure to be well translated into English. He offered me the copyright of all his works as a gift, and said he would give me carte-blanche to cut out all I thought necessary on my own account or that of the English public—and made out lists of how I had better arrange them, which he gave me.

‘ He sent me all his books, and was boyishly eager that I should set to work and read him some in English, especially a *prose* translation of his

songs, which he pressed me to undertake with the
greatest vehemence, against my opinion as to its
practicability.

'He talked a great deal about politics in the
same tone as in his later writings—a tone of
vigorous protest and disgust of mob-tyranny, past,
present, and future; told me a vast number of
stories about people of all sorts, which I should not
choose to repeat; and expressed the greatest wish
that it were possible to get well enough to come
over to visit me and effect a reconciliation with
England.

'On the whole, I never saw a man bear such
horrible pain and misery in so perfectly unaffected
a manner. He complained of his sufferings, and was
pleased to see tears in my eyes, and then at once
set to work to make me laugh heartily, which
pleased him just as much. He neither paraded
his anguish nor tried to conceal it or to put on any
stoical airs; I also thought him far less sarcastic,
more hearty, more indulgent, and altogether
pleasanter than ever. After a few weeks he begged
me not to tell him when I was going, for that he
could not bear to say, " Lebewohl auf ewig," or to
hear it, and repeated that I had come as " ein
schöner gütiger Todesengel," to bring him greetings

from youth and from Germany, and to dispel all
the " bösen französischen Gedanken." When he
spoke German to me he called me " Du," and used
the familiar expressions and turns of language
which Germans use to a child ; in French I was
" Madame " and " vous." It was evident that I
recalled some happy time of life to his memory,
and that it was a great relief to him to talk
German and to consider me still as a child. He
said that what he liked so much was, that I laughed
so heartily, which the French could not do. I
defended the ' vieille gaieté française,' but he said,
" Oui, c'est vrai, cela existait autrefois, mais avouez,
ma chère, que c'était une gaieté un peu bête." He
had so little feeling for what I liked most in the
French character that I could see he must have
lived only with those of that nation who " sit in the
scorner's seat ; " whereas, while he laughed at
Germany it was with " des larmes dans la voix."
He also talked a good deal about his religious
feelings, much displeased at the reports that he had
turned Catholic.

' What he said about his own belief and hope and
trust would not be understood in England, nor
ought I, I think, to betray the deeper feelings of a
dying man.

'The impression he made on me was so deep that I had great difficulty to restrain my tears till I had left the room the last few times I saw him, and shall never forget the pale sad face and the eager manner of poor Heine.'

Shortly before the end he wrote this last summary of the struggle of faith which had, as it were, possessed him during his existence, and never, I believe, in the strange tale of the poetic life has there been so wonderful a maintenance of imaginative power and intellectual integrity through long years of physical anguish up to the very gates of death.

———————

Full fell the summer moonlight in my dream
    On the wild shrubs that marked an ancient pleasaunce,
And richly sculptured stonework that might seem
    Fine relics of the time of the ' Renaissance.'

Fragments of porches, gurgoyles, gable-ends,
    From that half-Christian and half-Pagan era,
As the mixed shape of man and beast portends,
    Centaur and Sphynx, and Satyr and Chimæra.

Still here and there some Doric capitals,
    Topping the lofty thicket, make you wonder
How straight they rise when all about them falls,
    Gazing on Heaven as if they mocked its thunder !

But one sarcophagus without decay,
    And white as on the Roman's funeral's morrow,
Contained a coffin, wherein perfect lay
    A manly corse, wasted with pain and sorrow.
14*

This was upheld by Caryatides
   With outstretched necks and ever weary faces,
While bas-reliefs unfolded by degrees
   Scenes that filled up the marble's smallest spaces.

There the old powers that on Olympus dwelt
   Sunned their gay godships in unconscious beauty ;
There our first parents reverently knelt,
   Attired in fig-leaves from a sense of duty.

There was the tragic tale of burning Troy,
   Sweet Helen, and the shepherd who caressed her ;
There Aaron priest—great Moses, man and boy—
   Judith and Holofernes—Haman,—Esther.

There the god Amor, ever fair to see,
   Phœbus Apollo—Vulcan—Lady Venus,
Pluto, Proserpina, and Mercury,
   The garden-god, with Bacchus and Silenus.

Near them were Balaam, and his ass that got
   The power to talk like other human asses ;
And Abraham's horrid sacrifice, and Lot,
   Whose tipsy deed the very gods surpasses.

There too Herodias trippingly brought in
   The Baptist, or at least his head without him ;
And Hell flared out with Satan's hideous grin,
   And Peter bore the keys of Heaven about him.

Then, following round the sculptures as they ran,
   You saw the work of Jupiter's loose hours ;
Leda delighted with the downy swan,
   And Danae, revelling in the golden showers.

There wild Diana and her high-girt troop
   Chased the swift stag through open ground and shady,
And Hercules, forgetting his war-whoop,
   Sat spinning like a decent Grecian lady.

Then rose Mount Sinai, round whose sandy peak
   Its flocks and herds the pilgrim Israel gathers ;
Then stood the Child his mother went to seek,
   And found disputing with the grim old fathers.

Thus the sharp contrasts of the sculptor's plan
   Showed the two primal paths our race has trod ;
Hellas, the nurse of man, complete as man,
   Judea pregnant with the living God.

The ivy arabesques of green and gloom
   Hid all the rest ; when strangely up I started,
Conscious that that lone figure in the tomb
   Was I myself, worn out, and broken-hearted.

There at the head of my last couch was set
   A plant that grows in holy ground unbidden ;
Its leaves unburnished gold and violet,
   And a rare love-charm in its blossom hidden.

The simple people call it passion-flower,
   And in tradition's botany we find
It sprang from earth on Calvary, the hour
   That Christ's dear blood was shed to save mankind.

And for its own unchallenged evidence,
   Each bloom within its marvellous recesses
Bears symbols potent to the humblest sense
   Of all the martyrdom that word expresses.

Nature with dainty miniatures adorns
   Each calyx here in terrible remembrance—
The cross, the cords, the scourge, the crown of thorns,
   Cup, nails, and hammer, each retains its semblance.

Such was the plant my fancy deemed to stand
   Beside my open tomb; with vain endeavour
Touching my silent head, my useless hand,
   Kissing the eyelids that are closed for ever.

habits of a sparse and
striking contrast to the
Western neighbours, the
the last and former centu
of aristocratic possession
difficulties of transport
at the time of their cons
dered enormous, some o
decorated of English ma
of these isolated palaces,
is the most notable, weld
unexpected vicinage of a
viewer in the disguise of
competed for his society wi
of York, over the church
Harcourt, the last of the C
Establishment, so long pres

This intercourse not only
have been a sad change from
ities and frequent festivities
life, but increased that for
association with the represe
station in society which alon
or even tolerable, to his inde
demanded equality, at least,
entered, and generally got s

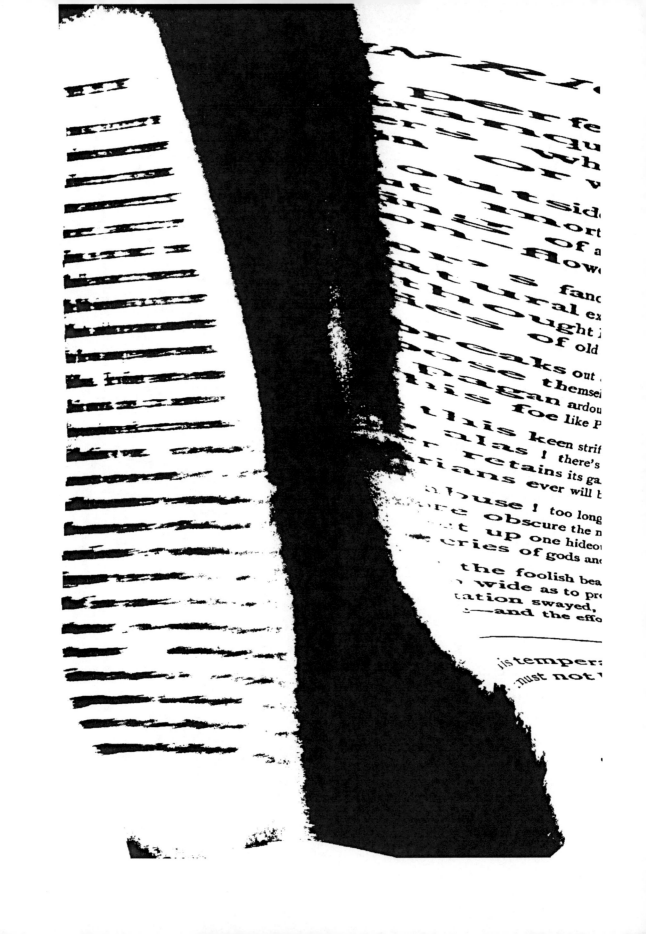

O witchcraft of the visionary life !
    That flower, by some internal grace transmuted,
Became thyself, my darling and my wife,
    Deep in the centre of my being rooted.

What odorous ichor can thy tears excel ?
    What sun-fed blooms can realise thy kisses?
That passion-flower was all the world's as well,
    But thou art all mine own, thou bliss of blisses !

Through my shut eyes I feel the gracious boon
    Of thy divine compassion bending o'er me ;
And clothed in ghostly lustre by the moon,
    Thy features glimmer solemnly before me.

We could not speak, and yet my spirit heard
    The thoughts and feelings welling in thy bosom :
There's something shameless in the uttered word,
    Silence is Love's most pure and holy blossom.

So all varieties of mental sound,
    From speechless gossip up to noiseless thunder,
Filled up the night's too transitory round—
    That summer night of rapture, pain, and wonder.

Oh ! never ask us what our dumbness said—
    Ask the mild glow-worm what it burns and simpers,
Ask the wild brook what's running in its head,
    Ask the soft zephyr what it breathes and whimpers ;

Ask what the diamond to the ruby gleams,
    What the night-violets murmur to the roses,
But ask not what the Flower of Sorrow dreams
    To him who in the moonlit grave reposes.

Alas ! my luscious ecstasy of peace,
    My cool sarcophagus, my mellow glory,
Were but a specious, incomplete decease,
    And not the finis of my vital story ;

Not death—that only perfect happiness,
  By whose sublime tranquillity we measure
This life which blunders while it tries to bless
  With aching passion or with tickling pleasure.

And now, it seemed, outside my tomb arose
  A storm that all but mortal slumber banished—
Sounds like the meeting of ancestral foes,
  At which my passion-flower affrighted vanished.

The forms the sculptor's fancy had devised
  Acquired a supernatural existence,
And mid the rage, I thought I recognised
  Familiar voices, cries of old resistance.

From the dry stone breaks out the war of creeds,
  The bas-reliefs dispose themselves for battle;
Pan's dying wail the pagan ardour feeds,
  And Moses blasts his foe like Pharaoh's cattle.

Ay ! evermore must this keen strife go on,
  Beauty and Truth, alas ! there's no uniting;
For while each power retains its garrison,
  Greeks and Barbarians ever will be fighting.

What curses ! what abuse ! too long to tell;
  What dogmas, more obscure the more one searches !
When Balaam's ass set up one hideous yell
  That drowned the cries of gods and prayers of churches.

Hee-haw ! hee-haw ! the foolish beast outbrayed,
  Opening his jaws so wide as to provoke me,
Till, by an angry imitation swayed,
  I brayed responsive—and the effort woke me.

These poems, this temperament of mind, even this
noble endurance, must not be judged by a Christian

standard. Although Heine had received his primary education from the Roman Catholic clergy who directed the public schools at Dusseldorf under the French occupation, and though he was afterwards formally received into the Lutheran Communion, probably for some political object, Heine never seems seriously to have assumed even the profession of the Christian life. He remained essentially a Hebrew, and was no inconsiderable example of the forms which the ancient genius has in modern times assumed. Israel sitting holy under his fig-tree and singing the praise of the invisible God, and exercising mercy and justice amid the bloody and dissolute rites of Babylon and Nineveh and Sidon and Tyre, was the highest image that his mind would contemplate; and in the institution of the Jubilee he finds an apology for the very Socialists whose advent he expects with terror. For him, it is the Jews who preserved the Sacred Writings through the bankruptcy of the Roman Empire; and the Reformers who revealed, and the perfidious British monopolists of commerce who are diffusing them throughout mankind, are but the unconscious founders of a world-wide Palestine. There is no more earnest passage in the whole of his writings than that in

his volume on Börne, where he observes on the
embarrassment of the old Greek grammarians who
attempted to define, according to recognised notions
of art, the beauties of the Bible—Longinus, talking
of its ' sublimity,' just as æsthetic moderns of its
' simplicity '—' Vain words, vain tests of all human
judgment. It is God's work, like a tree, like a
flower, like the sea, like Man himself,—it is the
Word of God, that, and no more.' We have seen
something among ourselves of this enduring sentiment of religious patriotism with interest and not
without respect. In Heine it was the saving element
of reverence which incurred the wrath of what he
calls the ' High Church of German Infidelity '—of
Bruno Bauer, of Daumer, and of Feuerbach—' who
did me too much and too little honour in entitling
me their Brother in the Spirit—of Voltaire.' That
he undoubtedly never was ; the wit of thoughts
preserved him from the tyranny of the wit of words.
The humour which abounded within him flowed
over the whole surface of nature, and left no place
for arid ridicule and barren scorn ; it fertilised all
it touched with its inherent poetry, and the produc-
tive sympathy of mankind manifests itself in the
large crop of his imitators who have sprung up, not
only in Germany, but other countries. Many a

page of modern political satire rests upon a phrase of Heine ; many a stanza, many a poem, germinates from a single line of his verses.   The forms of wit which he invented are used by those who never heard his name, and yet that name already belongs to the literature of Europe.   The personal tragedy of his last years adds a solemn chapter to the chronicle of the disasters of genius, and the recollection of the afflictions of ' the living Shade of the Champs Élysées' will mitigate the judgment of censorious criticism, and tinge with melancholy associations the brightest and liveliest of his works.

THE END.

TAINE'S WORKS.

I.—ENGLISH LITERATURE. A Cheaper Edition. Translated by H. Van Laun. Two vols. 8vo, cloth, $7.50; half calf or morocco, $12.50.

In every library, public or private, one of the first necessities is a standard work on Literature. The critics unite in giving the first place to Taine's English Literature.

"It is the best history of English literature that has yet been produced."—*Nation.*

"No English book can bear comparison with it for richness of thought; for variety, keenness, and soundness of critical judgment; for the brilliancy with which the material and the moral features of each age are sketched."—*London Spectator.*

"The delicate and sympathetic insight, the mastery of the subject, and the vivid and picturesque style—unparalleled in such a work—seem to me equally remarkable."—*George W. Curtis.*

"I consider it the best history of English literature in existence."—*Bayard Taylor.*

"I concur fully with the favorable opinion expressed concerning it by Mr. Taylor."—*Wm. Cullen Bryant.*

II.—A CONDENSED EDITION OF TAINE'S ENGLISH LITERATURE for General Readers and for Schools. Prepared by John Fiske, Assistant Librarian and late Lecturer on Philosophy in Harvard University. Post 8vo, $2.50.

This edition is just what is wanted by that large class of our people who would be glad to read the larger edition if they had the time.

III.—NOTES ON ENGLAND. Translated by W. F. Rae. With a Biographical Sketch and Portrait of the author. Post 8vo. $2.50.

"In acuteness of observation and sagacity of comment, he rivals the 'English Traits' of Mr. Emerson, while in freshness of feeling and warm human sympathies, he surpasses that remarkable volume."—*New York Tribune.*

"Excels all previous travellers' accounts of England and its people."—*Boston Commonwealth.*

IV.—ON INTELLIGENCE. Translated by T. D. Haye. 8vo, $5.00.

"We feel certain that it will be welcomed as soon as known by the most advanced school of English mental science. . . . . . The book deserves to be, and we hope will be, universally read by real students of Psychology."—*J. S. Mill, in the Fortnightly Review.*

V.—ITALY. (Rome and Naples; Florence and Venice.) Translated by John Durand. Two vols. 8vo, gilt side and top, $5.00; cheap edition, two vols. in one, plain, $2.50.

"M. Taine studies its (Italy's) art from its history, and not its history from its art, as Mr. Ruskin does, for example; and we think he has by far the clearer idea of the time, its people and its work."—*Atlantic Monthly.*

VI.—IDEAL IN ART. Translated by John Durand. 16mo, $1.25.

VII.—ART IN THE NETHERLANDS. Translated by John Durand. 16mo, $1.25.

VIII.—ART IN GREECE. Translated by John Durand. 16mo, $1.25.

IX.—THE PHILOSOPHY OF ART. Translated by John Durand. 16mo, $1.25.

This volume contains the course of lectures on the principles of art, which was preliminary to the other courses contained in the author's volumes on 'Art in Greece,' 'Art in the Netherlands,' and the 'Ideal in Art.' In the subsequent volumes 'The Philosophy of Art' is constantly referred to.

HOLT & WILLIAMS, Publishers,

25 Bond Street, New York.

Recent Publications.

THOUGHTS FOR THE TIMES. Sermons by the Rev. H. R. HAWEIS, author of "Music and Morals." 12mo, $1.50.

"He aims at nothing less than laying down the first principles of that new liberal theology which is to characterize what he calls the Church of the Future. Mr. Haweis writes not only fearlessly, but with remarkable freshness and vigor."—*Saturday Review.*

"It contains much to interest, entertain, and instruct; . . . [his] illustrations are always good."—*London Spectator.*

"They are very unlike the ordinary run of English sermons; . . . apart from the unquestionable cleverness . . . they have a special interest as exhibiting the treatment which old-fashioned orthodoxy is just now undergoing at the hands of the liberal clergy. The whole volume, indeed, bears marks of much originality of thought and individuality of expression."—*Pall Mall Gazette.*

BIOGRAPHIA LITERARIA. By SAMUEL TAYLOR COLERIDGE. Centenary Library Edition. 8vo, 2 vols., $5.00.

"The edition is very much more than a reproduction of Coleridge's own work, and its value to students of the place and influence of Coleridge in modern culture cannot be too strongly stated. The publishers have given it an elegant dress, and we have no doubt that they will receive the thanks of many of our younger students, who are now able to place among their choice books a very choice copy of a work so important."—*College Courant.*

LEGENDS OF THE PATRIARCHS AND PROPHETS. Current at the East, by the Rev. S. BARING-GOULD. Crown 8vo. $2.00.

"There are few Bible readers who have not at some time wished for just such a volume. * * * This is a thoroughly interesting book, and will be seized with avidity by all students of the Bible."—*The Congregationalist.*

"Mr. Baring-Gould has * * * had very good success in making books of entertaining reading, but we believe he has never succeeded better than in these Legends."—*Nation.*

"They have the magic charm of the Arabian Nights."—*Methodist.*

"It will be his (the reader's) own loss if he forgoes the pleasure of reading this entertaining volume."—*London Saturday Review.*

HISTORICAL COURSE FOR SCHOOLS. Edited by EDWARD A. FREEMAN, D. C. L.

The object of this series is to put forth clear and correct views of history in simple language, and in the smallest space and cheapest form in which it could be done. It is hoped in time to take in short histories of all the chief countries of Europe and America, giving the results of the latest historical researches in as simple a form as may be. Those of England and Scotland will shortly appear, and authors are at work on other parts of the plan.

1. **OUTLINES OF HISTORY.** By EDWARD A. FREEMAN, D. C. L. 16mo. $1.25.

2. **ENGLAND.** By Miss EDITH THOMPSON. *In Press.*

BAIN'S ENGLISH GRAMMAR. A brief English Grammar, on a Logical Method. By ALEXANDER BAIN, LL.D., Professor in the University of Aberdeen, author of "The Emotions and the Will," "The Senses and the Intellect," Treatises on Psychology, Logic, Rhetoric, etc. 18mo, boards, 50 cents.

HOLT & WILLIAMS, Publishers,
25 Bond Street, New York.

CPSIA information can be obtained at www.ICGtesting.com
226053LV00002B/152/P

9 781143 037504